STAY SHARP

STAY SHARP

Keep your brain active and banish forgetfulness

Published by The Reader's Digest Association, Inc.
London • New York • Sydney • Montreal

CONTENTS

Consultants

Professor Robert Logie PhD FRSE FBPsS FRSA
Centre for Cognitive Ageing and Cognitive Epidemiology,
University of Edinburgh

Sheena Meredith MB BS MPhil

Fiona Hunter BSc Nutrition Dip Dietetics

Resources

Note to readers

While the creators of this work have made every
effort to be as accurate and up to date as possible, medical and
pharmacological knowledge is constantly changing. Readers are
recommended to consult a qualified medical specialist for individual advice.
The writers, researchers, editors and publishers of this work cannot be held
liable for any errors and omissions, or actions that may be taken as a
consequence of information contained within this work.

Yes, you can CHANGE YOUR BRAIN

Congratulations! This is an extraordinary time to be alive. Modern medicine has developed cures and treatments for many of the health conditions that once felled us in our prime, giving us the most valuable gift of all: more years.

Wonderful indeed – but what kind of gift is extra longevity if our minds wear out before our bodies do? After all, the brain contains everything that makes us 'us': not only every talent and skill but also the records of all our experiences, our hopes and dreams, the jokes and friendships and births and achievements that give our lives purpose and meaning.

It's no wonder, then, that with every little 'brain hiccup' – forgetting a name, losing our car or house keys (again), a sudden losing streak in our regular bridge or whist game – we see our very lives slipping away. In fact, many people fear losing their memories more than they fear death itself.

The good news is that although the brain does shrink a little with age, its remaining capacity is still pretty large. This book was put together in consultation with some of the world's pre-eminent neurologists and psychologists, using hundreds of medical journal articles, and the message is positive.

It turns out that even with age most brains still retain the capability to learn and can continue to add new stores of information. Plus, a wealth of techniques have been discovered that can help you to make the maximum use of your mental abilities – you can effectively train your brain and improve the efficiency of your memory, whatever your age.

AGE AND EXPERIENCE

Another piece of good news: the common saying 'You can't teach an old dog new tricks' isn't true. Although ageing may have some effect on memory and learning capacity, the experience and knowledge store that age brings can compensate for much of this.

What's more, taking heed of the information in this book, including the memory-improvement techniques, can help to preserve your mental functions into old age. And any slips can often be countered quite easily, for example, using aids such as diaries, Post-it notes or electronic reminders.

EXPANDING OUR INTERESTS

As we age and our mental filing cabinets become packed full with the record of lives well-lived, the brain makes more complex associations between ideas and puts new learning in the context of a vast reservoir of experience. What this means is that it becomes easier to take in new information about topics of which we have some knowledge or experience. So someone who takes up stamp collecting as a hobby will gain more and more knowledge about stamp collecting and will find it easier to add to that knowledge.

The same is true of any area of interest, whether it is a hobby or a profession – football, rock music, playing bridge, choral singing, politics, birdwatching, medicine, psychology, astrophysics or television soap operas. And as well as helping to maintain your mental abilities, pursuing a serious new interest will make life more stimulating.

BRAIN POWER

There are more potential connections between the cells in a single brain than atoms in the entire universe. The brain has about 100 billion neurons (nerve cells), and each neuron has up to 1,000 'docking points' where it can connect with others. If all of these potential connections were made, there would be 100 thousand billion information-exchanging links. In practice, of course, only a tiny fraction of these connections are ever established.

TWO BREAKTHROUGHS THAT CHANGED THINGS

The brain, once a mysterious 'black box' that scientists couldn't decode, is finally revealing some of its biggest secrets, and the news offers huge promise to anyone who's ever wondered, 'Am I losing it?' High on the list are two major findings:

WE DO GROW NEW BRAIN CELLS

Who doesn't remember knocking back a drink in their youth and joking to a friend, 'Well, there goes another thousand brain cells'? Many of us still believe that we start life with billions of brain cells, then slowly lose them with time (and alcohol). That we'll have fewer brain cells by our twenties and thirties, and by middle age, well, heaven help us. But, in fact, in a remarkable discovery, scientists have learned that the brain generates new cells every day, in a process called neurogenesis.

Continued on page 12

QUIZ

HOW SHARP IS YOUR BRAIN?

Read each statement below. If it sounds like something you would be likely to say or that generally describes your experience, tick 'True'. If it does not describe your experience, tick 'False'. Before you begin, try to remember these three words: tree, basin, dinner.

1 My friends and/or colleagues joke about my forgetfulness.

☐ True ☐ False

2 If I'm introduced to someone, the chances are I won't remember his or her name an hour later.

☑ True ☐ False

3 When I'm having a casual conversation, I often find myself struggling to think of the right word.

☑ True ☐ False

4 When reading a book or long magazine article, I regularly have to go back and reread passages because my attention wanders.

☑ True ☐ False

5 It is not unusual for me to say, 'Could you repeat that more slowly?'

☑ True ☐ False

6 I sometimes worry about my memory.

☑ True ☐ False

7 My memory isn't bad; it might just take me a little longer to think things through.

☑ True ☐ False

8 I often misplace items I use every day (keys, pens, mobile phone, shopping list).

☐ True ☑ False

9 I don't trust myself to do even simple maths without a calculator any more.

☑ True ☐ False

10 I find it very difficult to add numbers in my head.

☑ True ☐ False

11 I couldn't function without a calendar or written schedule – I need something to remind me of important dates and appointments.

☐ True ☑ False

12 I have a lot of stress in my life.

☑ True ☐ False

13 It is not unusual for me to say, 'What were we talking about again?'

☐ True ☑ False

14 More than once a week, I forget why I went into a particular room or cupboard.

☑ True ☐ False

15 I do better if I focus on a single thing at a time – I don't like multi-tasking.

☐ True ☑ False

16 I don't like adding new electronics to the house – I've barely learned (or didn't learn) how to work the DVD player.

☐ True ☑ False

17 It feels as though the world is running at a much faster pace than I am – people seem to be constantly waiting for me.

☑ True ☐ False

18 It is difficult for me to hold more than three numbers in my mind.

☐ True ☑ False

19 My abilities in games of skill and strategy (for example, bridge or chess) would be better if my memory were better.

☑ True ☐ False

20 I routinely take more than three prescription medicines per day.

☐ True ☑ False

21 I have been diagnosed with Type 2 diabetes, depression or heart disease.

☑ True ☐ False

22 I smoke.

☐ True ☐ False

23 I quit smoking less than 20 years ago.

☐ True ☑ False

24 I can't seem to find enough time to exercise – twice a week is a lot for me.

☑ True ☐ False

25 I have a sweet tooth and eat sweets, cakes or desserts almost every day.

☐ True ☐ False

26 I often get lost, probably because of my poor sense of direction.

☑ True ☐ False

27 Thank heavens for speed-dial; I just can't seem to remember phone numbers any more.

☐ True ☐ False

28 People often tell me that I've already told them the same story or joke before.

☐ True ☑ False

29 When I go to the shops to get groceries or other items, I almost always forget something and have to go back.

☐ True ☑ False

30 It feels as though I go through life with the notion that a name or fact is 'on the tip of my tongue'.

☐ True ☐ False

31 I know what I want to do; I just have a difficult time working out how to accomplish my goals.

☑ True ☐ False

32 Organisation is not a strong point for me.

☐ True ☑ False

33 I often find it difficult to persuade people of my opinion, or to make a reasoned argument against someone else's opinion – my thoughts simply don't come out as organised as I want them to be.

☐ True ☐ False

34 I frequently 'get lost' while I'm watching a film or reading a book – plots seem to be much more complicated these days.

☐ True ☑ False

HOW SHARP IS YOUR BRAIN? Scoring

1 **Do you remember the three words you were asked to note at the beginning of this quiz?**
(No peeking!)

1 ....   2 ....   3 ....

Give yourself one memory point for each word you missed. If you got them all, your score for this question is zero.

My memory points: ....

2 **Count the number of True responses for questions 1 to 34. Add this number to your memory points. This is your general** *Sharp Brain* **score.**

My general *Sharp Brain* score: ....

If your score is 0: Are you sure you answered all of the questions honestly? Everyone has mental blocks from time to time, regardless of age or mental capacity. Perhaps you should have another go at the quiz?

If your score is 1 to 10: Now is the perfect time to begin taking care of your brain – before forgetfulness and fuzzy thinking become a problem in your life.

If your score is 11 to 20: Your minor memory problems probably pop up as little surprises in your daily life. You can benefit from brain training, along with a few lifestyle changes such as those suggested in Part 3.

If your score is 21 to 37: You probably feel as though your brain is betraying you. It is possible to reduce or eliminate many of your memory problems with the exercises in this book, along with making lifestyle changes such as those outlined in Part 3.

Note: If you get a very high score and find memory problems interfering with your life, it might be a good idea to ask your GP to check if you have an underlying problem that could be resolved.

- ⬤ **ATTENTION AND FOCUS**
- ⬤ **MEMORY**
- ⬤ **PROCESSING SPEED**
- ⬤ **VERBAL SKILLS**
- ⬤ **NUMBER SKILLS**
- ⬤ **REASONING SKILLS**
- ⬤ **LIFESTYLE/HEALTH ISSUES**

A clue to the colours

This quiz taps into six main facets of cognition: attention and focus, general memory, mental processing speed, verbal skills, number skills and reasoning skills. It also looks at some lifestyle habits that affect the brain. Keep your answer to each question handy; you'll look back at this quiz when you get to *Your Brain Fitness Programme* in Part 2. There you'll discover how to use the colour coding of the questions to learn more about your particular areas of strength and weakness.

IT'S RUBBISH!

Don't believe these three common brain myths.

MYTH 1 Our ability to remember declines with age.
THE TRUTH The older brain loses some agility, but still has plenty of storage capacity. Remembering a complicated set of directions or a long list of words will require more time and repetition. But if we put in the effort, we'll retain the information just as well as, if not better than, a younger person.

MYTH 2 Memories are precise photocopies of information or events.
THE TRUTH Memories are not stored. They are interpretations of events, reconstructed every time we call one up. They live in complex networks of nerve-cell pathways throughout the brain, which contain fragments of events and a lifetime of accumulated knowledge. Each reconstruction is a mixture of what actually happened and our brain 'filling in the gaps' based on 'what must have happened' from accumulated knowledge, so most recollections are not completely accurate.

When we commit something to memory, we are 'laying tracks' along a memory trail. Just like a woodland path, the more we walk down it, the more firmly established it becomes. However, we lose details of any one specific journey along the path, just as if, say, we go to the same restaurant many times. We may remember what usually happens there, but tend to forget details of individual visits.

MYTH 3 Our brains are less sharp from our forties or fifties onwards.
THE TRUTH Mental agility actually begins to slip from around the age of 24 for some skills, while others seem to get better in early adulthood, before starting to decline in middle age. The older we are, the harder we need to work to keep our brains functioning efficiently, but if we find ways to compensate by gaining expert knowledge and experience, or learning useful techniques, then our brains can outstrip even those of younger people.

What really happens is that most new brain cell growth continues until early adulthood, around the age of 18 to 20. Thereafter, new brain cells do grow, but more die off than are replaced, so there is a small and gradual but progressive overall loss of brain cells throughout the rest of adulthood.

The crucial point to bear in mind is that it's not the number of cells but the connections between them that count. Whenever you learn new things, you create new connections between the cells and thus increase the capacity of your brain. The activities outlined in *Stay Sharp* could even help to speed up that process.

THE MORE YOU USE YOUR BRAIN, THE GREATER ITS CAPACITY

The second major new finding is equally encouraging. We used to think of the brain as if it were a fixed electric power grid, like the many that send electricity to our cities. When the system gets old or overloaded, the power decreases, which leads to, for example, flickering lights and dead appliances. We believed that age wore down memory and comprehension in a similar way, and that there was nothing we or anyone else could do about it.

Today, we know that the brain can continue to adapt and expand its capacity as needed. Not only does it generate new brain cells but it also creates new connections between those cells in the form of intricate nerve fibres called dendrites. The more connections in your brain, the faster and better you think. The advice, strategies and exercises in *Stay Sharp* are designed specifically to help you to expand your brain's power grid.

USE IT OR LOSE IT

Whether you're balancing your accounts, learning salsa or playing gin rummy, your brain's 'electricity grid' lights up like Oxford Street at Christmas. Chemical messages zip along at speeds of up to several hundred miles per hour from one nerve cell to the next along 'cables' called axons. Waiting to receive all that information are the nerve cell 'branches' mentioned earlier, called dendrites. And guess what? You play the most important role in keeping this network humming.

'Learning new skills and new knowledge increases the number of connections in the brain, and the more connections there are, the more efficient the brain will be,' says Robert Logie, professor of human cognitive neuroscience at Edinburgh University. Forcing our brains to learn something new causes them to sprout more and more dendrites, expanding our capacity to think, decide, learn and remember.

On the other hand, being mentally lazy – getting stuck in a rut, never trying anything new – has the opposite effect. The brain, in constant clean-up mode, allows unused neurons to die and 'prunes' under-employed dendrites, just as a gardener prunes dying branches on a tree.

RICH REWARDS

Keeping our brains in tip-top shape may even protect against the decline in mental functioning that tends to occur with age. Many studies have shown that higher levels of leisure-related mental, physical and social activities are associated with better cognitive health in later life. Of course, it could be that the people who choose a more varied and challenging

BRAIN POWER

A small number of people possess what memory experts call 'total recall'. They can remember every detail – what they wore, what they ate, what the weather was like, who visited that day and so on – of any specific day from adolescence onwards. Such memory feats highlight the vast potential of the human memory.

lifestyle are those who are more mentally active to begin with. But taking up or increasing your level of activity does seem to confer benefits. A 2008 review commissioned by the UK government's Foresight Project, 'Mental Capital and Wellbeing', noted that cognitive training in later life could improve memory, reasoning and speed of information processing, and that the gains could be long-lasting, for at least five years. A multitude of other studies have reached similar conclusions. Here are three simple everyday ways to boost brain power:

● **Talking.** A study found that chatting for 10 minutes a day improves memory and test scores.

● **Walking.** In a study published in the *Journal of the American Medical Association*, researchers looking at data from the US Nurses Study, involving more than 18,000 women, found that long-term regular physical activity, including walking, is associated with significantly better cognitive function and less cognitive decline in older women.

● **Playing video games.** A study of people in their sixties and seventies found that playing a strategy video game, one that focused on world domination, improved cognitive skills.

YOUR SHARP BRAIN ACTION PLAN

What's the best way to nurture your neurological garden? Of course, lifestyle is important. Small tweaks to diet, exercise and sleep, as well as a healthy social life can help you to think more clearly, retain information more effectively and concentrate better. It can be something as simple as going for a brisk walk or taking an occasional class.

Your diet is especially important. A study published in *Archives of Neurology* suggests that following the Mediterranean diet can provide a powerful defence against mental decline. After five years, people who followed this diet – high in fish, fruit, vegetables, legumes and monounsaturated fats such as olive oil, moderate in alcohol and low in red meat and dairy products – had a 28 per cent lower risk of cognitive impairment.

Certain foods are more beneficial than others – oily fish, walnuts, pumpkin and flax seeds, for example, contain the omega-3 fatty acid so important for brain health; antioxidant-rich fruits such as blueberries, blackberries and cranberries are also recommended. Gaining abdominal fat and high cholesterol levels can be bad for your brain as well as your heart.

Exercise is good for your brain, not just your body, and simply getting adequate sleep can almost magically clear up fuzzy thinking. (The ability of test subjects assigned to memorise lists of words improved by 30 per cent after a good night's sleep.)

FIGHT THE FOES

There are certain other villains that can rob your brain of its power, and you may need to protect yourself. Some are the usual suspects: smoking and drinking to excess are just as bad for your brain as they are for the rest of your body.

Muddled thinking? Many of us can blame it on stress. In one study, stressed-out medical students performed markedly worse on an important exam. Depression can also rob us of brain power. When the blues turn black, the symptoms can include foggy memory, difficulty with comprehension, even slurred speech. In elderly people, these symptoms are commonly mistaken for dementia, but mental skills quickly bounce back when the depression is treated.

CROSS-TRAIN YOUR BRAIN

We've all heard the advice to take up crossword puzzles or play chess to keep the mind fit. That's a good starting point. It'll definitely make you better at crosswords or chess – but that alone won't help you find your car keys, says cognitive neuroscientist Robert Logie. Just as runners devote a portion of their training

BRAIN POWER

A 'happy' brain can help to fight off infection. The body's immune system responds directly to changes in the brain. A sad event – such as losing a loved one – can produce a measurable depletion in the number of infection-fighting blood cells within four days.

... soon you'll find that your brain has recharged and rejuvenated, and is ready to learn and remember.

to swimming and cycling, you'll need to vary your activities if you really want to keep your brain in prime shape.

Athletes call this cross-training. Part 2 of this book, *Your Brain Fitness Programme*, is designed to help you do just that. You'll discover a series of entertaining puzzles and exercises specially designed to challenge your brain in the six main cognitive areas mentioned on page 10: attention and focus, general memory, processing speed, verbal skills, number skills and reasoning.

Spend a few minutes on them every day, and you should notice improvements in your brain 'fitness' in no time. You'll also discover useful everyday strategies for everything from remembering phone numbers to recalling names that are always on the tip of your tongue.

There's evidence that intellectually curious people are more resistant to brain decline. They have what scientists call a cognitive reserve, which means they have more nerve cells and dendrites than others

to begin with. So if their brains eventually suffer damage due to a disease such as Alzheimer's, they're likely to function well for a longer period.

Bearing all this in mind, are you inspired to banish memory slips, chase away brain fog, sharpen up your concentration and focus, reduce your dementia risk and boost your self-confidence? You've come to the right place. This practical, comprehensive plan is based on the latest science, but promises to be an enjoyable challenge every step of the way. Try the puzzles and exercises, follow the advice, and soon you'll find that your brain has recharged and rejuvenated, and is ready to learn and remember.

As for losing your car keys, no one can guarantee it won't happen again. But you can rest assured that it's something we all do, regardless of our brain health. So instead of worrying, use your mental energies to find a designated spot to keep those keys. And develop a new habit of putting them back when you come home.

AN ODE TO WISDOM

When we're young, the only kind of intelligence that is valued is the kind that results in high scores in school exams. But in older people, different types of intelligence become increasingly useful and garner respect. It's about the depth of knowledge that can come only from experience. 'Sixteen-year-olds think they know it all and reject the advice of their parents, but when they themselves get older, they recognise the knowledge that comes with life experience and are puzzled as to why the young do not want to listen to their advice,' says Professor Logie. Wisdom isn't just about having an evolved opinion. Think of it as being 'streetwise' – in other words, older people's broader knowledge and experience enable them to put together different pieces of information more effectively.

part 1

YOUR AMAZING BRAIN

WHAT MAKES US TICK?

a brief brain tour

At first glance, the brain is less than impressive. It's a wrinkled grey mass whose surface resembles that of a walnut (that's because the brain folds itself up – just as your intestines do – to fit more matter into a small space). If you were to poke it, it would feel like a mound of soft tofu. Not very promising.

Appearances are deceptive, though: your brain is astoundingly complex and perpetually active. Even while you sleep, it isn't entirely at rest, carrying on its vital role of maintaining breathing, heartbeat and other bodily functions, and dealing with bursts of increased activity as you dream. When you're awake, the brain has truly amazing multi-tasking abilities. In an instant, it controls all your physical functions, with your senses sensing on full alert, all while you drive a 2-tonne vehicle at 70 miles per hour down a busy motorway, watching the road signs, remembering your route, digesting your lunch and listening to the radio. Not bad for a wobbly mass of grey matter.

How does it get it all done? You'd never know by looking at it, but the brain contains distinct regions, each with its own job to do. Much of what is known about how different parts of the brain work came from observing how people act and react after damage to certain areas due to injury, tumours, seizures or stroke. Now fMRI scans, which highlight brain activity, complement this valuable work.

GREY MATTER: WHERE IT ALL HAPPENS

The entire wrinkled outer layer of the brain is the cerebral cortex, also known as grey matter. Only a few millimetres thick, it contains 77 per cent of the total volume of brain tissue, much of it hidden in its many folds and convolutions. The cerebral cortex (see pages 22–23 for more information) is largely responsible for all forms of conscious experience, including perception, emotion, thought and planning.

The two sides of the brain – the left and right hemispheres – further divvy up these functions. Usually in right-handed people – and generally vice versa in left-handers – the left hemisphere controls language, while the right side controls art and spatial orientation skills. Writing a letter involves your left brain; painting a picture or finding your way back to your car in a crowded car park would be down to your right brain.

Because the body's nerves cross sides, the left hemisphere controls the right side of your body, and the right hemisphere controls the left. The two halves of your brain are connected by millions of nerve fibres bundled together in a thick cable called the corpus callosum. This 'bridge' allows the brain to merge and coordinate skills so it can act as a united whole.

An interesting aside: if the corpus callosum is damaged or severed, the two sides of the brain can't communicate. If an apple is placed in the left hand of a blindfolded person who's suffered this kind of brain damage, the right side of his or her brain would recognise it as an apple using smell and touch. But because the brain hemispheres aren't talking, the right side can't relay the concept to the language centre on the left side. It would be impossible for this person to come up with the word 'apple'.

COMPLEX NETWORK

Grey matter is not a single material but a biological construct of capillaries (which carry oxygen and nutrients throughout the brain), nerve cells (also known as **neurons**) and glia, the cells that support, feed and communicate with nerve cells. Its **nucleus** contains genetic material (DNA) and generates proteins to maintain the neurons.

If you suck away the glia, you are left with a communications network wired from billions of nerve cells. This lacy structure underlies everything in your physical, mental and emotional life.

Life depends on neurons passing messages to other neurons. The messages from one neuron are transmitted along a single fibre called an **axon** and received by a multitude of short branches called

BRAIN POWER

The brain is able to alter almost any body function. Heart rate can be slowed, the bowel relaxed and blood vessels opened or closed, just through thought. Simply imagining being warm, for instance, can increase the temperature in a person's fingers by more than 1°C.

YOUR BRAIN'S COMMUNICATION NETWORK

Every thought, idea and memory you have forges a unique electrochemical path among the billions of neurons in your brain.

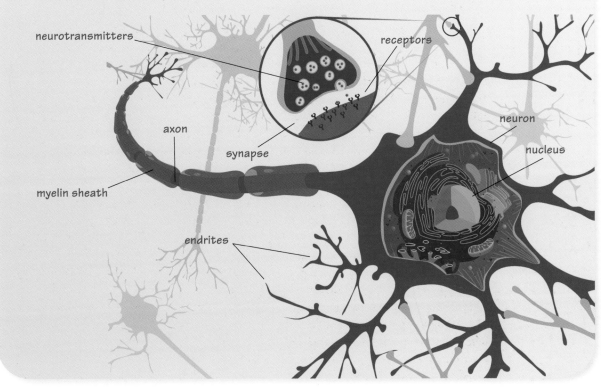

dendrites. As the information passes from one neuron to the next, it must jump across countless tiny gaps called synapses. This is where brain chemicals called neurotransmitters, such as serotonin and dopamine, come into play. When the information reaches the end of one neuron's axon, they carry it across the gap to receptors on the next neuron.

As with any communications network – think about your internet service provider, or mobile phone company and the satellites it uses to send information from one place to another – the better the network, the clearer the messages and the faster they are able to get through.

To transport information from one part of the brain to a more distant area, the brain uses special high-speed cables – bundles of axons coated by a fatty substance called myelin, which stands out from the rest of the brain and gives the brain's white matter its name. The coating insulates the bundles and speeds the transmission of electrical signals along this communication expressway, allowing for faster cognitive processing.

The brain can alter almost any body function.

YOUR grey matter AT WORK

We call brainy people cerebral for a good reason: the cerebral cortex, also known as grey matter, is where complex thought, attention and memory take place. Different functions occur in different areas.

① SHORT-TERM MINI-STORAGE The part of the frontal lobe closest to your forehead is the prefrontal cortex, the primary area for keeping short-term memories (also called working memory). Think of it as a temporary filing system that holds facts for just a few seconds – a phone number you are about to dial, for example. Thoughts or ideas reside here briefly unless you make the effort to commit them to long-term memory.

② DECISION MAKING, PLANNING AND PROBLEM SOLVING
The large portion of the brain called the frontal lobe is the brain's command centre. It controls decision making, planning, organising and problem solving. It also creates our personalities, sharpens our attention and keeps us focused on goals. It allows civilised societies to exist by putting the brakes on some of our baser instincts.

DAMAGE REPORT The 'caveman effect' Damage to the frontal lobe can result in wildly fluctuating emotions and difficulty performing even simple tasks. Think about it: just brewing a cup of tea requires dozens of individual steps, including finding the tea, filling the kettle, switching it on, waiting for the water to boil, pouring it into a cup, adding milk and more. Without planning abilities, this would be impossible to pull off

BRAIN P♦WER

The human brain has a built-in awareness of the thoughts of others. An intuitive grasp of other people's thinking and their view of situations develops in children at around the age of four. Before this age, children usually assume that others have the same information and feelings as themselves. This 'mind-reading' ability is located in the frontal lobe of the brain.

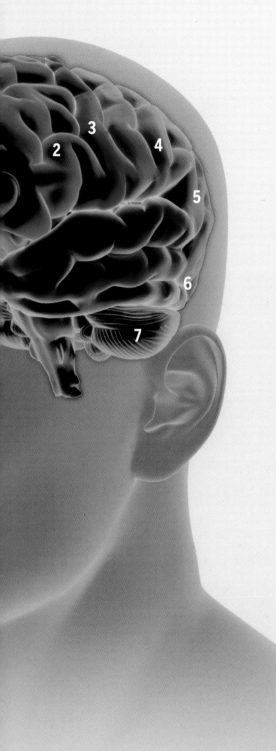

3 MOVEMENT At the rear of the prefrontal cortex is the primary motor cortex, controlling all movement. Brain scientists can now identify the locations in the motor cortex associated with distinct patterns of movement, such as the hand motions of musicians. In fact, it's even possible to know what instrument a musician plays by looking at changes in this part of the brain.

4 PHYSICAL SENSATIONS The parietal lobe, towards the back of the brain, is responsible for the body's physical sensations. A disproportionate amount of the parietal lobe is dedicated to some of the smallest – but most sensitive – parts of the body, such as the tongue, hands, face and genitals. The parietal lobe also plays a role in spatial recognition, language and our ability to focus attention.

DAMAGE REPORT *Half the story* Damage to the parietal lobe can distort the way a person perceives space and objects. If the damage is on the right side, the person may be totally unaware of anything on the left of his or her visual field, including the left side of a computer screen, the left side of someone's face or even his or her own left leg.

5 VISION The occipital lobe at the back of the brain manages vision. It controls eye focusing, interprets the meaning of all the shapes and colours we see, and records short-term visual memory.

6 REMEMBERING NAMES The temporal lobe, beneath the temples, connects to the ears and processes and interprets sounds. It also has a role in memory, particularly for words, ideas and names.

DAMAGE REPORT *Subtotal recall* If the temporal lobe is damaged, a person is unable to learn new facts or remember events. Life seems eternally new (and frustrating) because no new memories can be formed. A person with this type of damage could read the same newspaper over and over without getting bored.

7 COORDINATION AND BALANCE The cerebellum (the 'little brain') is a small wrinkled area at the base of the brain. Don't let its small size fool you – it contains half of the brain's neurons. While the motor cortex is the area that sends messages to the muscles, causing them to move, the cerebellum acts like a conductor, coordinating all the movements that let you successfully swim a length in the pool, knit a jumper or walk down the street.

DAMAGE REPORT *Drunk while sober* Injury to the cerebellum can cause dizziness, slurred speech, nausea and uncoordinated movements. Affected people are often mistaken for being drunk.

THE LIMBIC SYSTEM: BASIC INSTINCTS

Buried deep under the cerebral cortex is the limbic system, a set of primitive structures responsible for some of our most basic human instincts and drives. Craving a piece of chocolate cake? Blame, in part, the limbic system, which regulates our response to pleasure. Bolting down the street to escape a fierce dog? Thank the limbic system, which is largely responsible for our survival instincts. Terrified of bees after being stung badly as a child? The limbic system is the culprit, because it won't let you ever forget that event. Emotional memories are often subconscious, but they may suddenly pop up in the form of panic attacks or flashbacks.

The limbic system is also in charge of our most primal urges, including those of a sexual nature. Damage to this part of the brain leaves appetite, aggression and sex drive completely unregulated.

DÉJÀ VU?

The limbic system may be involved in the unique phenomenon we know as 'déjà vu' (literally, 'already seen'). This sense of having been in an unfamiliar place or of having had a conversation and lived through the moment before has been regarded by some people as evidence of reincarnation. Others have explained it as the memory of a dream in which the person 'experienced' the moment in advance of it happening. Conversely, the sense of 'jamais vu' ('never seen') occurs when what is known and familiar becomes for a while strange and unusual.

Scientists now believe that both are caused by a momentary failure of the limbic system to react appropriately. When déjà vu takes place, information flowing through the limbic system is mistakenly tagged with familiarity. When this incorrectly identified information merges with information from elsewhere in the brain, it produces a puzzling sense of familiarity. Conversely, in the case of jamais vu, the information's true emotional significance is not recognised as it should be.

NEW thinking

A brain in your belly?

What sends and receives information along a complex neural circuit, communicates with the help of chemical messengers called neurotransmitters (such as dopamine and serotonin) and is capable of functioning independently? Yes, it's the brain – but it's also the stomach.

The brain and the gut are intimately linked. For example, when you imagine something fearful or exciting, your heart rate increases and you get butterflies in your stomach.

Did you know that:

● An upset stomach can lead to a headache?
● Stomachs get their own form of 'migraines'?
● Antidepressants can calm the intestines of people with irritable bowel syndrome?

Some experts hypothesise that the brain in our stomachs may even hold sensory memories that we don't consciously recall, but which nonetheless guide us. Gut instinct? Maybe so.

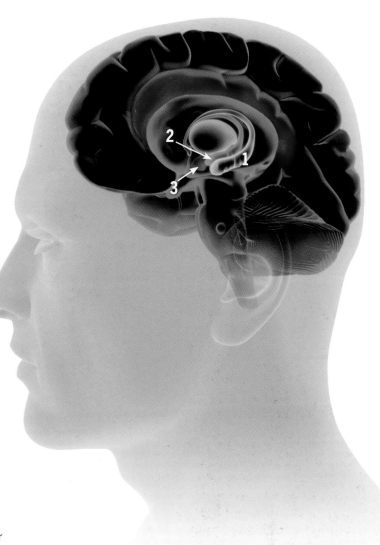

1 **THE HIPPOCAMPUS** This tiny area of the brain, whose shape first reminded scientists of a seahorse (*hippocampus* is Greek for 'seahorse'), converts short-term memories into long-term ones. It shares responsibility with the hypothalamus for aggressive behaviour, sex drive and appetite. And it's largely responsible for spatial memory and navigation. It's one of the first regions to become damaged in cases of Alzheimer's disease, causing memory problems and disorientation.

2 **THE AMYGDALA** This part of the brain helps to regulate fear, anger and sexual response. The old thinking was that it played a special role in processing emotional memory, taking highly charged events, such as a traumatic attack, a flunked job interview or a first kiss, and making sure they are stored permanently in your mind. The new thinking is that the amygdala may actually play a role in all long-term memory formation.

3 **THE HYPOTHALAMUS** Does your heart beat faster even when you just think about a scary upcoming event? Pehaps it's your driving test, an exam or an important meeting at work. That's the hypothalamus at work. About the size of an almond, this region has an amazing amount of control over what happens in our bodies, and even over our moods and actions. It not only controls sexual arousal and behaviour but also regulates hunger and thirst, sleep and wakefulness, responses to pain and pleasure, levels of anger and aggression, and even our body temperature, pulse, blood pressure and other physical responses to emotional events.

Some of our most emotional memories are triggered by scent. The olfactory system, which processes smells, has direct links to the amygdala – the group of brain cells now thought to help forge long-term memories. This may be why unusual scents from the past have such power to evoke vivid personal recollections.

MEMORY & LEARNING

Do you remember the geometry equations you learned in school? Can you still recite a poem off by heart? Do you recall what you had for breakfast last Tuesday? Some bits of information just seem to slip away, while others stick in the brain with startling clarity and little or no effort.

how they work

It's a good bet that you remember the words to the theme song of your favourite childhood TV programme, the exact time of day your children were born, the name of your favourite primary school teacher and the price you paid for your first house or car. Yet, no matter how hard we try, we are never totally in control of our own memories.

Cognitive neuroscientists, however, are gradually learning exactly what happens in the brain to allow us to process and record our experiences – and why some ideas, facts and images stay with us while others are destined to dissolve in the mist.

MEMORY: THE LONG AND SHORT OF IT

Certain kinds of information in our brains are captured and released without our even knowing it. Other types stick around very briefly, long enough for the knowledge to be used and forgotten – or, if we make an effort to learn it, transferred to longer-term storage.

HERE AND GONE: BELOW THE RADAR

Memory begins with experience, and we're drenched in a sea of experience every second of every day. There's no getting away from it. If you close your eyes, you can still hear. Block your ears and you can nevertheless taste. Shut your mouth and you can still smell. Hold your nose and you can still feel. Registering these sensory experiences is effortless and automatic – it doesn't even require your attention. Stop reading this book for a few seconds and look around the room. Without any conscious effort at all on your part, your brain is registering everything within the scope of your vision. This first level of memory is called sensory memory.

Memory begins with experience, and we're drenched in a sea of experience every second.

So where does all that sensory information go? Pretty quickly, it vanishes. If you look out of the window and see a bird alight on a branch of a tree, then fly away again, within just 60 seconds you wouldn't be able to point out which branch the bird had landed on. You saw it, your brain registered the information, but the sensory memory (the visual image of the bird on the tree) melted away.

While you may not notice sensory memory, it's essential for navigation, not to mention safety. (For example, it reminds you that a loud crashing sound indicates danger.)

The only way to hold on to these fleeting memories for longer is to pay conscious attention to the sensory input you receive. In the example of the bird, if you knew in advance that you'd be asked which branch it had landed on, you'd pay more attention, focusing on that bit of information and taking it to the next memory level – working memory.

brain HiCCUPS

Twin vanishing act

One of my silliest 'senior moments' happened on the second day of a new school year. I was running around frantically trying to find the twins' books, and make breakfast and packed lunches, while also dealing with the girls' anxieties about their new class. They had gymnastics after school, so I sorted out their kit – shorts, T-shirts, socks and gym shoes – wrote a note to the teacher that the twins were not to come home on the school bus, and reminded the girls three times that they had gymnastics that day.

When 3pm came round, I went to meet the girls at the bus stop. The other children got off as usual, but not the twins. I screamed, 'Where are my children?' My heart was pounding. The bus driver calmly called the school to ask about them. The school responded, 'They are at gymnastics.' Of course! I walked away, thoroughly embarrassed.

TEMPORARY STORAGE

Working, or short-term, memory, requires you to pay a bit of attention, unlike sensory memory. As you're reading this passage, you're using your short-term memory to remember the gist of the sentences that came before so that what you're taking in makes overall sense.

True to its name, short-term memory lasts for only a few seconds to a few minutes. Think of all the times you looked up a phone number, got briefly distracted before making the call, and had to find the phone number all over again. Not only is the storage time for working memory short, the storage space is small. For example, when scientists test working memory for numbers, they find that we can hold only about seven digits at a time – fewer, coincidentally, than the number of digits in many phone numbers. Of course, some people can remember eight or nine, but recalling more than that requires knowing and using specific strategies. (There's more about those in Part 2.)

BRIEF BUT VITAL

With only a small capacity and short storage time, what's the point? Actually, short-term memory plays a vital role in our daily lives. Those slivers of temporary information allow us to write down doctor's appointments, make everyday decisions and even have a conversation. Think about it: you have to recall what someone said to you 5 seconds ago in order to respond, though you don't need to remember it for ever.

This is information you use and forget – and good riddance. 'If we were to remember everything that we experience, our memories would rapidly become cluttered with lots of irrelevant detail. This would make it very difficult to recall specific details that we need to remember,' says Robert Logie, professor of human cognitive neuroscience at Edinburgh University.

Of course, it would be nice if some details didn't disappear before we could make use of them. When people say that they feel as if they are losing their memories, they are usually talking about short-term memory. Do you forget where you put your glasses or lose your train of thought during a conversation? Blame your working memory for those brain

WHY DO WE forget?

We all know lots of excuses for forgetfulness. When we say, 'I'm sorry I forgot your birthday because [insert reason here]', are we just making up a fake excuse? Here's a quick legitimacy check on the most common excuses:

Excuse	Truth?	
'I'm under too much stress.'	Yes	Chronic stress is like poison to the brain. Stress increases production of a natural steroid called cortisol, which damages the hippocampus– the brain's memory centre. Studies show that chronic stress reduces the efficiency of brain function and impairs attention, memory and thinking.
'I'm pregnant.'	No	There is no evidence that pregnancy itself has any effect on your mental clarity. However, if you are anxious about the pregnancy or about impending parenthood, this may affect your attention or memory.

Pregnancy itself has no effect on your mental clarity.

Excuse	Truth?	
'I'm going through the menopause.'	No	With apologies to women who feel blitzed by the menopause, the decline of oestrogen that marks the menopause does not cause much – if any – change in memory or cognitive function. (If you're not getting enough sleep, that's a different story.)
'I'm on a diet.'	Yes	People intent on losing weight quickly often put their bodies into a state of near starvation. Memory and thinking suffer as the brain is deprived of necessary glucose (blood sugar). Very low-carb diets can also make you feel tired, light-headed and headachy.
'I'm having chemo.'	Yes	Cloudy thinking in chemotherapy patients is so common, there's even a term for it: chemobrain. The medicines themselves can act like a brain-rattling smack on the side of the head. Chemo side effects, such as anaemia, fatigue, insomnia and worry, can also make concentration difficult. And one often-neglected cause is poor nutrition, as patients frequently lose their appetite.

hiccups. And yes, this function does tend to weaken with age. In fact, all of those so-called 'senior moments' may be related to a decline in working memory. But as you'll discover shortly, the more attention you pay in the first place, the better the information will stick.

LONG-TERM STORAGE

To keep information for days, months or even years, we need to consolidate it into long-term memory. And here's the good news: our brains have an unlimited amount of long-term memory storage capacity. The filing cabinet never gets filled up.

Of course, long-term memories can and will fade with time if you don't revisit them every so often, but the potential is there to remember them for ever.

The brain stores three main types of information in the long-term:

● **Words, facts and numbers.** When you're struggling to recall the name of the star in a film, the number of feet in a mile or the author of *Treasure Island*, you're wrestling with semantic memory. In Part 2, you'll find some tricks for improving this type of memory.

It can take up to two years for a memory to become permanent. Experiences that are being processed for storage as long-term memories may be replayed in the mind for up to two years. Once a memory is consolidated in this way, it has the potential to last a lifetime.

● **Events.** Episodic memory – think episodes – involves events or scenes from your life. Storing the general details of major events is effortless. You don't need to work at remembering what it was like to watch your daughter get married or how you felt the day you got your university place; you just do.

Certain exhilarating scenes, particularly around life milestones, such as a first kiss or the first day of a job, simply captivate us – and stick around. We also remember unpleasant experiences without effort. No one forgets being robbed, cheated or fired, for example.

But we do tend to forget specific details of even the most important events in our lives. You'll remember if you were robbed, but you might not remember the face of the thief, and there are numerous examples of mistaken identity, with, for example, an innocent bystander being identified as the criminal. The Alfred Hitchcock film *The Wrong Man* tells a true story of exactly this kind of event.

We also tend to forget details of more mundane events in our lives. What did you do on March 29, 2009? Unless that date was important in your life, it is unlikely that you will be able to remember more than where you were living and what kinds of activities dominated your life around that time.

● **Physical skills.** They say you never forget how to ride a bike, and it's true. You can thank a form of long-term memory called procedural memory, also called muscle memory. It's responsible for acquired habits and motor skills, such as the ability to play an instrument, drive a car or even tie your shoes (something else we never forget how to do). You acquire these skills through practice.

PLAY BALL – BUT START YOUNG

When older people are asked to memorise lists of words or numbers, they often do as well as younger adults. But some things – especially those that involve muscle memory – are simply easier to learn when we're children. Encoding new physical memories becomes more difficult as we get older, which means that it's much harder to learn to play an instrument, take up a new sport or learn sign language. It can be done, but it will take longer and require more effort.

Learning to play an instrument is easier when you're young.

If you ever learned how to play the guitar, for example, you'll remember how difficult it was to get your fingers into position to play a chord. But finally, after hours and hours of practice, those subtle hand motions became second nature, and your fingers went straight to their proper positions. Even years later, without practising, the chances are that you could quickly find the G chord.

Muscle memory is stored throughout the brain, which makes it virtually immune to the factors that cause us to lose information memories. That's why Alzheimer's patients retain their basic motor skills even when the disease robs them of the ability to recall a family member's name.

PROSPECTIVE MEMORY

Have you ever forgotten to post a letter, pass on a message or turn up for an appointment? Everyone experiences these everyday failures of 'prospective memory', or remembering to do things. It might be that you put a letter by the front door intending to pick it up on your way out but forgot to do so a few minutes later, or you might intend to make an appointment for the dentist later in the day but come the evening the appointment has not been made. Most of the time we do remember to do things – turn up for work, take our children to school, buy food for dinner or meet up with a close friend for coffee. But, without prospective memory, it would be very difficult to function in our daily lives, and might even have serious consequences: for example, if we forgot to take medicine or check the cooker when deep-frying chips.

HOLD THAT THOUGHT – BUT HOW?

All this talk about memory storage makes it sound as though there is some kind of brain warehouse just waiting to be filled; the metaphor has even been used of a memory filing cabinet when describing the brain's capacity to keep information in the long term. Yet no such cabinet or warehouse exists. Cognitive neuroscientists have searched for decades to find it, with no luck. So where exactly do memories live – and how do they get there? Even more important, how do we make sure they stay there?

CREATING A MEMORY

Science now suggests that long-term memories aren't stored in a single place but, rather, in vast networks of nerve-cell pathways. Every recollection begins as a 'spark' in the brain triggered when we receive input from our senses. This spark becomes an electrical signal as it travels from neuron to neuron. Each memory

Ask the
MEMORY EXPERT...

My husband can drive or be driven somewhere once and remember the route months later, even if it's in a distant part of the country. I, on the other hand, continue to get lost in my own city unless I follow a known route. Is there a sense-of-direction centre in the brain? Or does he just have a better general memory (even though he can't remember to buy milk)?

PROF. ROBERT LOGIE: Men do seem better than women at learning and recalling directions and orientation – which involves the right parietal lobe and other areas of the brain. Women tend to be more skilled at reading human emotional cues. But there are many exceptions to such general findings with, for example, outstanding female navigators and very empathetic men. Different people, different talents.

forges a unique pathway among the billions upon billions of neurons in the brain, as if blazing a new trail through a dense forest.

As the information passes from one neuron to the next, it jumps across gaps called synapses, with the help of neurotransmitters, such as serotonin and dopamine. Neurotransmitters are vital to memory – and, unfortunately, we produce less of them as we age. But by continuing to challenge our brains to learn new skills and information, we can create more and more dendrites, which help keep our brains young and sprightly.

Work hard enough or for long enough at a given type of memory and your brain will grow and adapt in other ways, too. In an astonishing 2000 study, London taxi drivers, who spend their whole careers learning to navigate one of the largest, most-convoluted road systems in the world, underwent MRI screenings of their brains. The cabbies were found to have unusually large hippocampuses, an area of the brain that plays a major role in memory formation, particularly spatial memory. What's more, the longer someone had been driving a taxi, the larger their hippocampus – an association not found in bus drivers, who drive set routes, according to a later study. This suggests that acquiring a specific expertise, in this case complex navigational skills, can actually cause structural changes in the brain.

MAKING IT STICK

Some memories naturally tend to persist better than others, but you can help any memory to stick by following these two simple strategies.

1 Pay attention.

The first step in remembering something is paying attention to it. Unless you seize information by focusing on it, it can slip right past you.

HOW A *fact* IS LEARNT

Step 1

We perceive Sights, sounds, sensations, tastes, smells. Our brains take in this information whether we pay attention to it or not.

Step 2

We focus If we focus on the information, it gets moved into the working memory. If we don't, the information fades within seconds.

Step 3

We rehearse With enough repetition, study and review, the fact gets moved to the long-term memory. Otherwise, the fact placed in the working memory dissolves.

Can't recall the name of someone to whom you were just introduced? You probably weren't paying enough active attention to the name (maybe you were focused on smiling and looking friendly). Most people find it easier to remember faces than names, partly because even in a short conversation you spend, perhaps, 5 minutes concentrating on the face, especially one that you find particularly attractive or unattractive, compared with seconds to register the person's name. The trick is to link recognition of the face, which is generally easier, with the more difficult task of recalling the name.

You may notice that people who are good with names often repeat the person's name out loud. If they meet someone called John Robinson, for example, they may say, 'Good to meet you, John.' Silently, they may be making an association: 'John is from Switzerland: Swiss Family Robinson.' By repeating it, then making the effort to come up with a rhyme, a reference or an association, they create a nerve-cell pathway – a memory trail – in the brain for the name, so it doesn't vanish without a trace. You'll find more tricks for making names stick better in Part 2.

2 Practise and repeat.

Consolidation is the process of making a nerve-cell pathway more permanent. Each time you review or revisit a fact, each time you repeat it, the pathway becomes a little stronger. This is what we typically think of as learning.

The likelihood of consolidating any particular fact or memory depends on a number of factors, including what you want to learn (whether it's a fact or a skill), your current knowledge base, your emotional state, and how well you take care of yourself. The work of consolidation is also easier if you have a background that relates to whatever it is you are trying to learn, just as it is easier to keep track of an invoice or important tax form if you have an existing file folder for this exact type of information than if you throw the paper on the desk and vow to remember its location later.

Inexperienced chess players who look at pieces on a chess board, for example, will find it very difficult to recall where all the pieces have been placed. But chess champions can remember the placement of the pieces quite easily because they have an excellent knowledge of the game. Rather than just seeing individual pieces set up randomly, they see the strategic challenges illustrated by the set-up of the board, and that puts the information in context, permitting better recall.

Similarly, a fascinating study by Robert Logie at Edinburgh University and his colleagues Richard Wright and Scott Decker at the University of Missouri, St Louis, USA, showed that thieves are more likely than others to remember the details of houses that might be relevant to a burglary, such

NEW thinking

We remember useful information better.
Information is easier to recall, especially as we get older, if it makes sense and seems useful. In typical tests of memory, researchers ask subjects to recall lists of random numbers or words. But psychologist Alan Castel, PhD, assistant professor of psychology at the University of California, Los Angeles, and an expert in memory and cognitive ageing, tried something different. He asked his human guinea pigs to memorise lists of grocery items as well as their associated prices. The pairings were either unlikely (for example, loaf of bread: £8.71) or likely (such as, loaf of bread: £1.50). Younger people outperformed the older people at remembering the unlikely pairings, but older folk redeemed themselves when the prices made sense. Implication: in effect, older adults have learned to compensate for the normal decline in working memory by not wasting time on useless information. 'They focus on information with high value and discard the rest,' says Dr Castel.

as whether or not there is an alarm or a 'beware of the dog' sign. Which all goes to show that if you take the time to practise something (however dubious), your memory in that particular area of expertise will improve.

MAKING IT STICK BETTER

Certain emotional states (such as depression), lack of sleep and even certain medicines can make it harder to consolidate memories. As mentioned on page 14, getting enough exercise, keeping your social connections alive and eating brain-healthy foods can help you keep your brain skills at their peak.

A flashbulb memory is the brain's way of taking a mental 'picture'.

FLASHBULB MEMORY: PERMANENT SNAPSHOTS

Every so often, the daily routine of our lives is broken by the shock of an event so surprising, so monumental, that we remember every detail of where we were and what we were doing when we heard the news. Can you recall exactly where you were at the moment you learned about the September 11 attacks on New York's World Trade Center or the death of Princess Diana or Elvis Presley? Even years later, most of us have memories so vivid that recalling those tragic days can feel as if we are looking at well-preserved photographs. The same thing can happen to an even greater extent with very personal events, such as seeing a bad car accident or being bitten by a vicious dog. Psychologists call these intense impressions flashbulb memories.

As the name suggests, a flashbulb memory is the brain's way of taking a mental 'picture' of a significant emotional event. Because they are so vivid, accessible and durable, they become cognitive landmarks that allow us to place other, less dramatic events into a before-or-after context.

WHY IT IMPACTS

The closer a significant event hits home, the deeper the memory is embedded. Researchers from New York University interviewed 24 people who were in Manhattan at the time the World Trade Center's Twin Towers fell, and watched brain activity light up on scans as the they recalled their experiences that day. Some participants were within blocks of the Twin Towers, some were about two miles away, and others were more than four miles away. All had strong recollections of the day. But the strongest flashes, indicating the deepest, most searing kinds of memory, appeared only for those who were at or near the World Trade Center.

In forming these flashbulb memories, the hippocampus (which plays a major role in long-term memory) gets help from its immediate neighbour, the amygdala, which leaps into action when triggered by stress hormones such as adrenaline to process the memory quickly. These hormones prompt the amygdala to send messages to the brain that this is important and you'd better remember it. What's more, with events such as major disasters, 'flashbulb memories' result not only from an emotional response at the time but also the effect of 'practice and repeat'.

'At the time of a major event, there is massive news coverage on television and in the newspapers,' says Professor Robert Logie. 'It is the major topic of conversation with friends immediately

BRAIN POWER

When we first view a scene or situation, we rely on memory to help us make sense of it. The eyes see only a tiny part of any visual scene clearly. They dart around taking in more and more information, and memory enables us to assemble this sequence of fragments into a scene.

MEMORY TIPS FROM A
police expert

How many times a week do you try to recall a fact that stubbornly eludes you, like where you put the car keys? If only you could push a button to access the information. It's not that simple, but you can help yourself remember better with techniques that Natalie Sweet, a police composite sketch artist, uses with crime witnesses. Every day she helps ordinary people remember enough physical detail to create a meaningful portrait of a criminal suspect. Here are her tips.

Step 1 Try to relax.
If you've lost your keys, don't panic. That will only makes things worse.

Sweet takes the pressure off by telling witnesses that the purpose of a sketch is to come as close as possible to the person in their memory. It is not intended to be perfect, and no one will be arrested based on the sketch alone.

Step 2 Cast your mind back, picturing any details you remember.
Close your eyes and try to remember the last time you had your keys. Were you coming from a meeting? What were you wearing? Was it raining?

Sweet gives the witness's brain a chance to 'warm up' by talking over everything about the day of the crime, except the crime itself. For example, she might ask a man to go back in his mind to that day and remember everything that happened before the incident. Does he remember what he was doing immediately before? What was the weather like?

Once the witness seems relaxed, Sweet asks him to close his eyes and start describing what he remembers about the environment during the crime. She asks him to look around the room and describe everything he sees, such as what's hanging on the walls, the type of lighting and the colour of the walls.

Step 3 Pretend you were an onlooker.
If you had your keys when you walked into the house, imagine watching yourself enter. Are the keys in your hand? Did you linger on the doorstep?

Memories of any incident can be blocked by emotions, such as fear or anger. So Sweet gets witnesses to picture the scene as an onlooker would.

'I take them out of whatever position they were in, victim or witness,' says Sweet. 'I tell them to think of it as though they were standing outside looking in, as though they were filming what happened, or watching it on TV. It gives a different perspective.'

Step 4 Be flexible as you try to remember.
Replay the incident backwards and forwards until your mind finds a clue that leads to the critical image: where you put your keys.

Our brains have remarkable abilities to revisit our memories, backwards and forwards, from above and in freeze-frame. The memories are there – but we have to be flexible in how we hunt for them. After the witness describes the scene and event, Sweet asks him to 'rewind' the 'mind movie' to the place where he has the clearest picture of the suspect. Then, she asks him to freeze-frame it in his mind.

Step 5 Don't rush yourself. Let the memory come to you.
You will eventually remember; have patience.

Creating a sketch takes an average of 2 hours. Some take considerably longer. Mostly, you can't rush memory and expect good results.

Ask the
MEMORY EXPERT…

Why does my mind sometimes go blank when I try to introduce people I know perfectly well? This happened once when I was shopping with my best friend, and met another friend. I looked at the two of them, realised I couldn't remember either of their names, and finally said, 'Would you two please introduce yourselves?' Why did this happen?

PROF. ROBERT LOGIE: The information was encoded firmly in your brain; the problem was with retrieving it. It could be that spotting your other friend surprised you, or you worried about how to handle the situation, and the emotion temporarily jammed your retrieval system. This is totally normal.

Now, here's the bad news: because this has happened to you and the experience was embarrassing, any situation that requires introductions could become a source of anxiety. Then, the brain 'jam' could happen again and again. It is an everyday form of stage fright. Like any actor, try to rehearse your 'lines' as you see the scenario about to unfold, and you'll be fine.

following the event and for several days, if not weeks, afterwards. So there is a very large amount of repeated recall over an extended period, and this in itself can guarantee a vivid memory.'

Flashbulb memory is also influenced by expertise and interest in a subject. In a study Professor Logie and colleagues conducted with Professor Martin Conway (now at the University of Leeds, West Yorkshire), they found that interest in politics was a major factor in whether people had flashbulb memories a year after they heard the news that Margaret Thatcher had resigned as the UK's prime minister. People with a serious interest in politics, regardless of their political views, could remember very accurately what they were doing just before they heard the news, who they were with, and a host of other details normally forgotten.

People with a limited political interest didn't have these kinds of vivid memories, nor did people outside the UK.

RECALL ON DEMAND

Once the new tracks of a memory are laid down and reinforced by focus and repetition, you still need a way to recall it. If memory is a path in the woods, retrieval is finding the correct path. But there are hundreds of billions of different pathways. Most people worry when they can't locate a specific recollection, but given the vast multitude of pathways in our heads, the real mystery is how we ever manage to remember anything at all.

'It's a matter of retracing our steps, and feeding in other general information that we have,' says Professor Logie. 'Recalling memories is basically "reconstructing memories". But the route to a piece of information you want isn't a straight line. We use cues and associations to help us navigate through the memory pathways. If you cannot remember the name of the actress who played Iris Murdoch as she progressed into Alzheimer's disease in the 2001 film, for example, the first thing that might come to mind is that Jim Broadbent was her co-star, then that Kate Winslet played the young Iris in the film. Next you might recall that the actress also played "M" in later James Bond films, and this finally – aha! – triggers the memory for the name Judi Dench. In the brain, that roundabout circuit could be completed in a split second. You'd probably not even be aware that it was a path-finding process at all.'

WHY MEMORY IS FALLIBLE

As much as we would like to think that our recollections are accurate 'photographs' of events, they are more like impressionist paintings. Here's why.

● **Perception.** We all remember events differently because we perceive them in different ways in the first place. At your last family reunion, did you have a bad cold? If so, perhaps you remember the food as tasting rather bland, while your sister thought it was the best dinner she'd had for a while. Were you sitting at the end of the table, or in the middle? Your location affects which conversations you hear. Your sensory memory is unique and can never be replicated by anyone else, and it strongly colours your version of reality.

● **Interpretation.** If your uncle gave a long, impassioned political monologue, how you remember it will depend on whether you agreed with his viewpoint. If your cousin made an observation about a new exhibit at the museum, you're more likely to remember it if you believe your cousin knows what she's talking about. Your emotions, experiences and memories will all cause you to interpret events in your own unique way, and therefore skew how you remember them.

● **Recall.** Memories are not set in stone. The process of calling up the information from its disparate locations in the brain sometimes requires the brain to fill in blank spots. Consider this story: a woman was going through a family photo album with her mother. They came to a picture of a young girl on a pony, and the woman launched into her vivid memory of that day. 'But, darling,' her mother said, 'that's your sister. You weren't even born then.' The woman had seen the photo previously, assumed it was her, and her brain had filled in the details.

brain HiCCUPS

Missing the point – and the car
I needed to drop off my car at the garage for a minor repair in the middle of the day. My colleague Amanda offered to follow me to the garage, then take me back to work. Another colleague said she would come too. At the appointed time, we met at Amanda's office. Then we all got into her car and set out for the garage. When we were nearly there (gabbing the whole way), Amanda asked if I needed a ride back to the garage later to pick up my car. We both suddenly spun round and cried, 'We don't have the car!' We laughed so much that she nearly drove off the road.

WISDOM, CREATIVITY & INTELLIGENCE

the mechanics

Chemical reactions, electrical impulses, grey matter, neurons – this is the language of neurologists. They can explain the brain inside and out, from cells to lobes to hemispheres and back. But what about the elusive questions human beings have been asking for millennia about intelligence, creativity and wisdom?

What is intelligence? Where does creativity come from? What makes us truly wise? The answers don't lie in any single neuron or any single nerve pathway or any single place in the brain.

To understand these complex issues, we have to rely on psychology to make the connection between the physical brain and the intangible mind. While we may never be able to solve all of the brain's mysteries, experts are hard at work piecing together theories to explain these higher-order cognitions. In other words, they are thinking hard about the whole thought process.

INTELLIGENCE: NOT JUST A NUMBER

In psychological circles, the nature and essence of intelligence has generated more theories than the origin of the universe. The debate didn't start with the invention of the infamous IQ (Intelligence Quotient) test, but that method of measurement certainly ramped it up. Since then, the discussion – who's clever? Who's not? Does intelligence come from our genes? – has become one of the most heated of academic disputes.

Over 100 years ago, the psychologist Alfred Binet devised a test of intelligence quotient, or IQ, as a means of identifying which students would benefit from extra help at school. Over the ensuing years, society latched on to IQ as a precise measure of overall intelligence. But, of course, there's much more to intelligence than one number could ever suggest. (Albert Einstein's IQ may have been estimated at 160, but it's well known that he failed his university entrance exams the first time he took them, for example.)

NATURE OR NURTURE?

Researchers have theorised that intelligence is entirely inherited … entirely developed … 50 per cent inherited and 50 per cent developed. Some say intelligence is found all over the brain, others that it exists in specific brain locations only … that it includes more than 60 different abilities or is a single entity, or that cognitive intelligence is a subset within a more global general intelligence … that it is the single factor responsible for thought or that it is just one of many different cognitive abilities.

Whatever the truth, research does suggest that intelligence is relatively stable throughout someone's lifespan. One study by Professor Ian Deary and colleagues at the University of Edinburgh traced more than a thousand people born in 1936 whose IQ had been measured at age 11 as part of the Scottish Mental Survey in 1947. When they gave these individuals the same test at age 70, they found a strong correlation between childhood IQ and cognitive ability in later life.

This influence was far stronger than that of other factors, including people's own educational or occupational attainment and their fathers' social class. But neither intelligence nor background ensure either success or happiness. What also counts, it seems, is what we do with that intelligence and how much effort we put into exercising it during our lives.

As the researchers conclude, 'though social background may provide opportunities for educational and occupational attainment, the individual must embrace and pursue them in order for the effects of those opportunities to be realised. In fact, it may be that individual action has the strongest effects on late life cognitive function.'

This strongly suggests that learning new skills and knowledge, as well as using the various methods of improving your memory demonstrated in this book, can help your brain to work much more efficiently as you get older. There are many ways to develop and maintain your brainpower over the course of a lifetime.

brain HiCCUPS

Wrong number

I did something so stupid the other day when my friend left his mobile phone on my kitchen table. I knew he would miss it because it's the only phone he uses. So I called him to remind him that he had left it behind. It gave me such a scare when the phone on my table rang.

What's clear also is that there are different forms of intelligence, ranging from the erudition of a professor to the physical genius of the athlete. 'Not all intelligence is in the head,' writes Harvard professor Howard Gardner, explaining his mission to explore, identify and define its specific realms. After years of analysis, and using a strict set of criteria, Dr Gardner identified a total of seven intelligences. To find out what they are, see 'The Seven Intelligences' on pages 44-45.

It's a good bet that another sign of intelligence – one we could actually see, if ever a sufficiently sensitive method of brain imaging were invented – would be the number of neuronal connections throughout the brain. Given that neurons can increase their connections, theoretically, it should be possible to increase intelligence well into old age.

FROM INTELLIGENCE TO WISDOM

Intelligence includes the capacity for understanding and reasoning as well as the ability to learn and to use what is learned to reach your objectives. Although we value intelligence, the real measure of a person lies in his or her wisdom. Intelligence is raw and unripened. Wisdom, on the other hand, has been called the epitome of human excellence, an ancient and virtuous quality. If intelligence is knowing how to build a bomb, wisdom is knowing how to build a bomb, understanding the ramifications of using it, and being able to solve problems in such a way that the bomb is not needed.

Cognitive neuroscientists distinguish what they call 'fluid intelligence' – our ability to solve problems, think creatively and deal with novelty – from 'crystallised intelligence', which applies to the knowledge and experience that we accumulate over a lifetime (what might be considered as 'wisdom'). Whereas fluid intelligence does reduce somewhat during adulthood, starting in the early 20s, crystallised intelligence generally improves with age.

Continued on page 47

Who's clever? Who's not?
Does intelligence come from our genes?
The academic debate remains heated.

THE SEVEN intelligences

To deconstruct what we commonly describe as intelligence is to recognise that every person's contribution to society is unique – and valuable. No one person has all the skills or the learning needed to accomplish society's tasks, but together we are complete. Think of the different intelligences as colours, which can stand alone or be combined, made stronger or lighter, intensified or subdued. It takes only red, blue and yellow to create the entire spectrum of colour. Just think what could be created by the seven intelligences.

1 LINGUISTIC intelligence

Brain location Left hemisphere in right-handed people (often the reverse in left-handers)

Who has it most? Poets, writers, orators, many lawyers

What it's good for Just about everyone can speak, but some people elevate language to an art. Some of Winston Churchill's speeches come to mind. This type of intelligence is also displayed by writers and every silver-tongued devil you've ever met. Shakespeare is arguably the ultimate genius in this category. The average English-speaker uses 4,000 words. Shakespeare had a working vocabulary of 29,000 words. He also coined more than 1,700 new words, including many we use today, such as 'amazement', 'gloomy', 'zany' and 'equivocal'.

Recipe for improvement Doing a lot of reading can definitely build your vocabulary and lift your linguistic skills.

2 LOGICAL-MATHEMATICAL intelligence

Brain location Frontal and parietal lobes

Who has it most? Scientists, engineers, statisticians

What it's good for Even our common expressions recognise the genius of the science whizz: 'He's a rocket scientist!' You might almost call this the classic form of genius; it's the kind of intelligence that would show up on an IQ test. People with high levels of logical-mathematical intelligence can gather and consolidate information quickly. They tend to be methodical and organised.

Recipe for improvement Many of the puzzles in Part 2 help to strengthen logic as well as number skills. Give them a try. And practise your everyday number skills by calculating in your head rather than on your calculator.

3 SPATIAL intelligence

Brain location Right hemisphere in right-handed people (often the left hemisphere in left-handed people)

Who has it most? Sculptors, airline pilots, architects, theoretical physicists

What it's good for At its most basic level, spatial ability means being able to get from your house to the supermarket and back without being confused. But people who are really gifted seem to possess an internal GPS system that tells them precisely where they are in the universe at all times.

Recipe for improvement Look for puzzles that ask you to envisage how a piece of paper with patterns on it will look when folded to form a box. Beyond that, your best bet may be to buy a GPS.

4 INTRAPERSONAL intelligence

Brain location Temporal lobes

Who has it most? Philosophers, psychologists, theologians, writers

What it's good for Intrapersonal intelligence is about self-knowledge, being fully in touch with your inner self – your emotions, beliefs and the precise tremor and bias of your moral compass. High intrapersonal intelligence allows us to navigate through the world without losing our sense of self, to rebound from setbacks, and to appreciate fully our fellow human beings.

Recipe for improvement Keep a diary. More important, look with a fresh eye back on pages you wrote long ago and reflect on what they tell you about yourself.

5 INTERPERSONAL intelligence

Brain location Frontal lobes

Who has it most? Salesmen, teachers, social workers, good managers

What it's good for People with strong interpersonal skills understand non-verbal communication and are able to read the character, emotions and desires of others. This is a unique form of problem-solving that is not as easily measured as other types of intelligence, but is critical to social success. All good leaders are interpersonal geniuses. These gifts can also be used for dark purposes by con artists.

Recipe for improvement Practise noticing other people's reactions to your words, your body language, your tone of voice. Then try reading other people by noting their body language and tone.

6 MUSICAL intelligence

Brain location Right hemisphere (or often the left in left-handed people)

Who has it most? Composers, musicians

What it's good for Music is a form of communication, crossing countries, cultures and even species – birds and whales are just two species that speak through 'song'. People with high levels of musical intelligence can find meaning in the rhythm, tempo, pattern, pitch and tone of music. They often show signs of musical ability early in life and seem to grasp intuitively the mathematics behind the notes. Some can pick up an instrument and play it with barely any training; it's as if they instinctively know how to speak the language of music. At the

other end are those who avoid karaoke bars like the plague, the ones you'll find silently mouthing the words to 'Happy Birthday' to keep from throwing everyone else off-key.

Recipe for improvement A talent for music is something you either have or you don't, so it's difficult to improve. But learning to play an instrument can't hurt.

7 PHYSICAL intelligence

Brain location Motor cortex

Who has it most? Athletes, dancers

What it's good for Although movement comes naturally to just about everyone, exceptional physical grace and athleticism involve their own kind of intelligence. Controlled movements are expressive and productive – consider that one of the common tests of intelligence in other species is whether they have the ability to use tools. We are fascinated by dancers and awed by superior athletes. Conversely, we often good-naturedly mock those who are lacking in coordination skills.

Recipe for improvement Some people are simply more physically gifted than others. But staying active will keep your sense of balance intact and improve your posture, which helps to impart physical grace.

How wise ARE YOU?

To get an idea of where you stand on the wisdom spectrum, read each statement below and check the appropriate response.

1 I often reminisce about my past and am amazed at how far I've come.
☐ True ☐ False

2 Teasing is never appropriate.
☐ True ☐ False

3 Everyone is capable of dishonesty and hypocrisy.
☐ True ☐ False

4 I wear my emotions on my sleeve – if I'm upset, anxious or sad, people know it.
☐ True ☐ False

5 Before an election, I like to hear what all the parties stand for before coming to a decision about how to vote.
☐ True ☐ False

6 When I think back to my most embarrassing moments, I still feel mortified.
☐ True ☐ False

7 History is most interesting for what it can teach us about our lives today.
☐ True ☐ False

8 I think it's important to form a strong opinion – waffling is a sign of weakness.
☐ True ☐ False

9 I easily adjust my emotions to fit with the needs of the moment – it's not always necessary to let people know when I'm upset, anxious or sad.
☐ True ☐ False

10 I make decisions effortlessly, often on gut instinct.
☐ True ☐ False

11 I enjoy having religious discussions with people of different faiths.
☐ True ☐ False

12 If someone told me a lie, it would change my opinion of that person for ever.
☐ True ☐ False

13 I have experienced a lot of change in my life, and not all of it was positive.
☐ True ☐ False

14 History is interesting as a story, but has little relevance to my life today.
☐ True ☐ False

15 I have opinions, but I am always interested in hearing other points of view.
☐ True ☐ False

16 When I try to express my emotions, I often lose control.
☐ True ☐ False

17 I laugh easily and often.
☐ True ☐ False

18 I quickly become annoyed when people challenge my opinion.
☐ True ☐ False

19 I take my time before making a decision, often consulting many sources of information.
☐ True ☐ False

20 I have lived a charmed life, without much conflict or many dilemmas.
☐ True ☐ False

21 I've lived through a lot, and I've had to make some difficult and uncomfortable decisions.
☐ True ☐ False

22 I'm a happy person – I never feel angry or annoyed.
☐ True ☐ False

23 It's easy for me to laugh at my most embarrassing moments.
☐ True ☐ False

24 I hate it when people have a laugh at my expense.
☐ True ☐ False

25 Teasing can be a sign of affection.
☐ True ☐ False

26 My life has turned out exactly the way I thought it would.
☐ True ☐ False

In some ways, wisdom is like beauty – we value it, we desire it, we know it when we see it, but it is nearly impossible to pin down such an ethereal quality. Yet researchers have tried.

In the late 1980s, the Berlin Wisdom Project at the Max Planck Institute for Human Development in Germany set out to define it. They came up with the following qualities, all of which a person must have to be considered truly wise.

✔ Intelligence and factual knowledge.
✔ A deep understanding of human nature, including an empathy for people who are different or from other cultures.
✔ Emotional resilience, or the capacity to rebound from a setback.
✔ Humility.
✔ The ability to learn from experience.
✔ Openness, or the maturity to be comfortable allowing the world to see you as you really are.
✔ Superior judgment and problem-solving skills.

Put this all together and what do you have? A portrait of someone who's been around the block. Wisdom accrues from experience, so it's fair to say, you need to be older to be wise. However, it should be pointed out: not all older people are wise. There are plenty who are painfully blinkered and set in their ways and their thinking.

In 2007, the psychologist Jeffrey Dean Webster, of Langara College in Vancouver, Canada, updated the work of the Berlin Wisdom Project, adding the notion that true wisdom could be measured only by what you did with it, both in terms of self-knowledge and the improvement of society at large. In other words, wisdom is there to be used. Webster's Self-Assessed Wisdom Scale (SAWS) on page 46 measures what he considered to be key traits of a wise person, including open-mindedness, the ability to control emotions, sense of humour, experience and the ability to learn from the past. How do you rate?

PRACTICAL WAYS TO WISE UP

Almost everyone has the capacity to become wise, given the right mindset and a little effort. Wisdom requires a baseline of intelligence, but true wisdom is a mixture of balance (the ability to see all sides of an

SCORING
Count the number of **TRUE** responses for **ODD-numbered** statements: ....
Count the number of **FALSE** responses for **EVEN-numbered** statements: ....
To get your Wisdom Score, add those two numbers together: ....

INTERPRETING YOUR SCORE
0 to 4 Babe in the woods Best not to wander off alone
5 to 9 Student Keep watching and learning
10 to 14 Professor Wiser than most
15 to 19 Leader People depend on your guidance
20 to 26 Guru Consider setting up shop on top of a mountain

MIND versus MACHINE

How does the human brain compare with a personal computer? See for yourself.

	COMPUTER		HUMAN BRAIN	
Processing speed	60,000 million – or more – instructions per second	✓	About 100 million instructions – per second	
Work time	Unlimited, as long as plugged in	✓	Varies by person, but the brain tires relatively easily	
Memory capacity	A powerful desktop personal computer may have 1 million megabytes		Unlimited	✓
Memory accessibility	Every megabyte is potentially accessible at any moment	✓	Can be difficult at times	
Computation	A 2GHz processor can calculate the value of pi to a million decimal places in 1 minute	✓	30 million times slower than a computer	
Accuracy	Excepting a bug, computers are 100 per cent accurate	✓	The human brain makes many errors in all aspects of calculation and memory	
Adaptability	Once started on a processing problem, can't change unless redirected by a human		Can change direction, task and action in an instant	✓
Creativity	Works on a binary system for processing information – either yes/no or on/off		With at least 100 trillion neuron synapses, unlimited inventiveness is possible	✓
Energy efficiency	Computers use about a billion times more energy than the human brain		Low energy needs – oxygen and glucose (blood sugar)	✓
Multi-tasking	Can work on multiple problems simultaneously and perform equally well on all	✓	Can work on several tasks at once – breathing, thinking, walking, chewing, etc. – but can focus directly on only one problem at a time	
Learning	Computers are programmed; they can't learn on the job unless the specific program enables them to do so, in a limited way		Capable of learning from birth until death	✓
Free will and wisdom	No consciousness; no free will; can't learn, so incapable of wisdom		Has consciousness and free will; can determine its own destiny; has vast potential for wisdom	✓
Imagination	Computers have no ability to dream or indulge in make-believe		The human imagination knows no bounds	✓

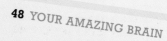

issue), open-mindedness, discipline and a concern for the greater good. There's no short cut to wisdom, but these strategies will lead you down the right path:

● **Read the newspaper.** You cannot make balanced choices unless you understand world circumstances and the experiences of others. If you don't already read a daily paper, start by going through a single front-page article, from start to finish, every day. Don't just scan or skip around it; read every word. Eventually, try to get through the main articles of a full newspaper every day. Most newspapers post their stories online, so you can have access to news from around the world virtually any time you want.

● **Find time for books.** While current events are important, both fiction and non-fiction books can help you expand your world view and allow you to explore new ideas and points of view.

● **Stay social.** Studies show that people who stay connected to others demonstrate higher levels of wisdom than those who are more isolated. Make an effort to join a club, sign up for Facebook, or invite an old friend or a new neighbour for coffee. And next time you're at a party or gathering, single out someone who's standing alone and start up a conversation. It's easy. Ask questions. ('Where are you from?' 'What kind of work do you do?') People generally love to talk about themselves. You, on the other hand, have the harder job: to listen closely.

● **Practise being more open-minded.** Wisdom is being able to understand all sides of an issue without letting emotions or personal feelings get in the way. Being open-minded means finding empathy and realising that everyone has a life story that influences their actions. During the course of every day, make a note of issues that get you hot under the collar, and take a moment to try to see the issue from the other side. No one needs to know.

● **Boost your self-knowledge.** You've learned a lot just by being alive, but have you taken the time to review all that you've learned? Try this exercise: write down your three biggest failures and your three greatest successes. For each, review the events that led up to it and what lessons you took away from the experience. Look for patterns. This is not a time for regret or pride; the goal is to learn to look at each experience, good or bad, as more fuel to enrich your wisdom.

● **Learn how to say these four important words: 'I could be wrong.'** A wise person understands that it is impossible to know everything and that life is capable of taking unexpected turns. Recognising your errors can lead only to greater wisdom – and admitting that there are times when you could be mistaken will go a long way in solidifying your reputation as someone whose advice can be trusted. As the Roman philosopher Cicero said, 'Any man is liable to err; only a fool persists in error'.

TOTALS... COMPUTER 6   HUMAN BRAIN 7

AND THE WINNER IS... **The human brain** – which also created and programmed the computer and harnessed the energy that drives it.

Ask the MEMORY EXPERT…

When I left home one morning, I set off on my usual route to work and when halfway there realised that it was a Saturday and I had intended to drive to the DIY shop instead as I needed to collect some paint for the bathroom we were redecorating. I obeyed all the traffic rules, stopping at junctions, signalling and allowing pedestrians to cross but could not remember doing any of this and was unaware that this was not the correct route today. How can the brain get us to carry out such complicated actions without us being able to remember or realise that we are going the wrong way?

PROF. ROBERT LOGIE: You had completed the journey to work so many times that you were on autopilot. If we carry out the same actions many times over, we can do them almost without thinking. The network in your brain for the route is firmly established, and if the journey goes as normal, it does not use much of your conscious attention. If there had been a dramatic event, such as someone stopping very suddenly in front of you, or a diversion because of new roadworks, your brain would change to 'control' mode rather than 'automatic' mode. Being in automatic mode can be helpful for working efficiently, but it can also lead to everyday slips such as forgetting that you had actually intended to go to the DIY shop.

> We often overlook the importance of creativity in everyday life.

EVERYONE CAN BE CREATIVE

Creativity is the most magical of the brain's skills. We trust that knowledge can be acquired and that wisdom will come to us with age. This seems to be true, according to Professor Logie. Fluid intelligence (see page 42) appears to be present at birth and has a major impact on how quickly we can learn. As people acquire skills and knowledge they gain new kinds of intelligence – or wisdom – linked to what they have learned. But creativity seems to be a gift bestowed upon only a few blessed individuals. It has proven more difficult to study than intelligence or wisdom.

Because creativity comes in flashes or floods, then dries up seemingly on its own, it is difficult to harness and nearly impossible to measure. As researchers from the University of Sydney, Australia, noted: ultimately, the only proven test for creativity is the creation itself.

Nevertheless, psychologists have uncovered some interesting facts about creativity. First, it's more evenly distributed than originally thought. Yes, some people are born with more creative gifts, but just about anyone can develop and nurture creativity at any age. Verdi, for example, composed his opera *Otello* aged 73 and *Falstaff* at 79.

Because creativity involves novel ways of thinking, it flourishes wherever originality is valued and individuals are encouraged to challenge traditional thoughts and styles. In other words, if you want to practise out-of-the-box thinking, you have to, well, step outside of the box.

LETTING GO MAY BE KEY

What is the 'box' that often holds us back in our adult life? One view is that the primary limitation on creative expression is expectation. We expect or wish to be successful. We wish to make others laugh. We wish to please. But what if creativity surfaces only when you relinquish your expectations and start existing in the moment, like a child? Children play just to play, not to impress anyone. Consider then that creativity is simply about making a deeper connection with your creative force, surprising yourself, and letting go.

Creativity goes hand-in-hand with the arts – music, dance, theatre, film, writing, painting – but we often overlook its importance in everyday life. It is this ability that allows us to generate solutions to problems, to hold fresh conversations, and to plan for the future. For example, throwing a surprise party requires finding a creative way to spring the actual surprise. And plenty of us show remarkable creativity when it comes to talking our way out of a parking ticket or justifying to a partner why we simply had to buy yet another pair of shoes/set of golf clubs.

Creativity is just as strong in older people, but sometimes we have to be prompted to remember that it's OK to play the way we did when we were younger. Studies show that older people who are involved in creative activities are more likely to remain connected to the community, to suffer less debility over time, and to live generally healthier lives.

FINDING YOUR CREATIVE SPARK

Creativity is about stretching your mind and coming up with solutions to unusual problems. To flex your creative muscle, try these exercises.

● Set a timer for 2 minutes and write down all the words you can think of that begin with the letter 'A'. Tomorrow, do the same for the letter 'B', and so on throughout the alphabet.

● For each of the following sentences, imagine what happens next. (There are no right or wrong answers.)

1 A woman wearing a red hat knocks on the front door of a large, extravagant stone house. When the door opens …

2 A man and a woman are out on a date, holding hands as they walk down a crowded city street. The woman looks up and gasps because …

3 A young man moves to a new country with his family, but worries that he won't fit in and will never find friends. To his surprise, on the plane over, the person seated next to him …

How your
BRAIN AGES

As we get older, our knees start to creak, our skin starts to sag, and our brains start to ... shrink? That's right: between the ages of 20 and 70, brain weight and blood flow to the brain drop by 20 per cent. And the total number of fibres and nerves in the brain decreases by 37 per cent. Sounds scary?

Maybe, but the news isn't nearly as bad as you may think.

Many of these types of changes exert effects that are subtle, if they're noticeable at all. Most of us are still capable of learning – and remembering – most things at just about any age, though it may take us a little longer.

In addition, it's easy to compensate for any small cognitive losses that do occur. For example, just as wearing glasses can make up for a decline in vision, using the memory strategies described in Part 2 can compensate not only for declines in short-term (working memory), but also for declines in episodic memory and in prospective memory (remembering to do things that you had intended to do).

Do you want to take up the trombone at the age of 76? You can. Would you like, finally, to read the classics you always said you'd tackle some day? Go for it. Everything you learn to do in the rest of *Stay Sharp*, from spending time in the 'brain gym' to getting more exercise (which increases blood flow and promotes the formation of new brain cells and connections), will help you keep your brain as young as possible.

AN HONEST ACCOUNTING

People over the age of 40 often worry about the state of their memory. We can be very hard on ourselves: one missed appointment, a forgotten phone number or two, and we panic. The truth is, most of us forget where we put things because our lives are too busy, we're trying to multi-task, we're too stressed or we didn't get enough sleep – not because we're losing our marbles. Some of us can also chalk up memory problems and dull thinking to medical conditions, anything from migraine to early onset Alzheimer's.

We tend to expect a lot from our memory – maybe more than it actually needs to deliver. Page 13 of this book mentions a rare group of adults with total recall of every single day of their lives from adolescence onwards. Name a date, and these people can tell you what day of the week it was, what the weather was like, whom they met and what they ate that day. Would you want this kind of memory? Probably not. In fact, some of those who possess this talent describe it as more of an exhausting curse than a blessing.

Likewise, we may admire the sponge-like memories of children, but it would be a mistake to feel at a loss because we can't absorb new information as quickly as they can. Consider this: most of us don't worry that we can't turn cartwheels or jump over fences in a single bound any more. Children not only have amazing physical prowess, their little bodies, still malleable and forming, can do things most adults wouldn't want to try without a chiropractor standing by. Like our bodies, our brains have also changed, becoming slightly less agile – but who really cares, as long as we can still perform the tasks we need to?

WHAT GETS WORSE

So, what is normal for an ageing brain? Researchers tell us that we can expect slight declines in the following four areas.

● **Short-term memory.** For reasons that science has not been able to pinpoint, our short-term memory, also called working memory – the type that enables us to remember what we are doing from moment to moment – generally gets worse with age. Older adults have fantastic long-term memories, able to recall details about childhood friends, the town they grew up in, and films they saw during secondary school, but they may

IT'S NOT ALL DOWNHILL

As with most things in life, getting older means you win some and you lose some. Here's the score card:

Usually better with age
● Long-term memory
● Emotional memory
● Untimed memory tests
● Wisdom

Generally worse with age
● Short-term memory
● Timed memory tests
● Speed of processing
● Reaction time
● Focus
● Multi-tasking

Usually no change with age
● Creativity
● Memory for important information

Short-term memory for what something looks like – the colour of a book you just read, say – starts declining in the early 20s.

forget whether they just swallowed the blue pill or the white pill, or whether the car that passed them a few seconds ago was green or red, or where they put down their glasses just moments earlier.

There are different kinds of short-term memory for visual and verbal material. Short-term memory for what something looks like starts declining in the early 20s – what colour was that book I just read, or where did my golf ball land? In contrast, short-term memory for verbal material – words, letters and numbers, for example, or remembering the sequence of a phone number until you dial it – tends to improve during adulthood and, assuming there is no underlying dementia or other problem such as depression, does not start to decline until well into retirement, when it drops off at a much slower rate.

Short-term memory is a temporary memory pathway that lasts only a few seconds and does not involve growth of dendrites, the connections between nerve cells. To grow connections in order to retain information, you need to pay attention to it and actively try to learn it. However, if you know a great deal about a topic, this will boost your short-term memory for information related to that subject. Professor Peter Morris at the University of Lancaster showed this in a study with soccer fans. When they were given the scores of real matches, they were extremely good at recalling them. But they were no better than soccer novices at remembering random scores.

So, while working or short-term memory capacity for information that is new and unrelated to something you know about may deteriorate with age, if you develop an expertise, your short-term memory for information related to that subject will improve. And the more expertise you gain as you get older, the better it will be.

● **Episodic memory.** When we have multiple memories of similar events or places, our brain creates related pathways that contain information specific to each particular event or episode. This is episodic memory and, in time, memories of each event merge to become part of our self-knowledge – for example, of the town we grew up in or the face of an old

We tend to expect a lot from our memory – maybe more than it actually needs to deliver.

friend. Such long-term memory for facts, known as semantic memory, is generally retained with age. But we are likely to remember specific details from a single occasion only if it was important to us – our wedding day, or the day we moved into a new house, for example.

Memories of other occasions tend to fade – you are unlikely to remember what happened on an ordinary weekend ten years ago or what you had for breakfast on the first Tuesday in June 1995. And such episode-specific information tends to get lost more often as we get older – so you may not remember what you had for breakfast yesterday. This explains why older people can usually remember events from their distant past, but often cannot remember what they did a few days ago.

The good news: although visual short-term memory and episodic memory tend to decline with age, as does prospective memory (remembering to do things in future), semantic memory – or knowledge – improves as we get older. This can often compensate for the declines in visual short-term and episodic memory.

● **Focus.** We also lose some of our ability to focus our attention, a problem that might mean it takes longer to read a book. We are more easily distracted by competing cries for attention, so reading a book with the television on can be challenging for some, impossible for others. Older adults also have a harder time multi-tasking.

● **Speed.** As we get older, our reaction time and the speed at which we process information both slow down. This means that not only do our brains sift through information more slowly, but our bodies also react more slowly.

It is important to be vigilant and make sure, for instance, that these normal changes don't affect your ability to drive or perform other tasks that require split-second reactions. In those cases, it's best to understand that slowness isn't necessarily an impediment. But most of the things we do are not potentially life threatening.

In timed tests of knowledge, younger adults do better than older adults, but take away the time factor and older adults do better. You can compensate for any slowdown by allowing more time to learn and remember things that matter to you.

PACE YOURSELF

Most of us can deal with learning a little more slowly as we age or having to turn off the TV while we're trying to read. Our real fear is that the little brain hiccups we all experience are the first symptoms of Alzheimer's disease or another form of dementia. This kind of worry may be worse than the actual forgetfulness.

But these are the facts: only about 5 per cent of men and women aged 65 to 74 have Alzheimer's disease. The numbers do go up after 75, to 16 per cent, though experts are not sure why there is this increase with age. But dementia doesn't necessarily have anything to do with being old, and not everyone who lives until old age will develop dementia.

The brain changes that take place in dementia are quite different from those of normal, healthy ageing. This is one reason why the word 'senile' is a far from accurate term for memory decline, as the root meaning of the word literally refers to old age. Instead, scientific experts have divided memory decline into three broad categories: normal age-associated forgetfulness, mild cognitive impairment (MCI) and dementia.

● **Those annoying brain hiccups.** Age-associated forgetfulness describes the normal state of having brief 'senior moments', when your short-term memory becomes weaker and, well, shorter. By the age of 60, about 40 per cent of us will experience this problem.

What causes it? As mentioned earlier, neurons shrink and die off, which decreases the number of synaptic contact points – those all-important brain-cell connections. We also produce smaller amounts of the brain chemicals called neurotransmitters, which allow communication to take place, and reduced levels of the hormones that support healthy brain function. Blood flow is reduced in all portions of the brain, but most strikingly in the frontal cortex, which is where our thinking, planning and speaking abilities reside.

This is a normal part of ageing, no worse than that mild ache you may feel in your knees. These age-related brain changes explain why we forget that appointment or have trouble coming up with the right word during a conversation. Mild forgetfulness is all part of the normal wear-and-tear of ageing, much of which can be compensated for.

● **When it's more serious.** Unlike the everyday forgetfulness described above, mild cognitive impairment suggests have memory problems that they simply can't cover up. These problems are serious enough to be noticeable to others and significantly change their ability to function in the world. They may forget how to cook, have trouble dressing themselves, and feel lost even in familiar surroundings.

Some dementias can be reversed, particularly if they have been caused by dietary deficiencies, a medical disorder (such as diabetes, depression or liver disease), or a side effect of a medication. Alzheimer's disease and similar types of dementia are irreversible today – though

Mild forgetfulness is a normal part of ageing, no worse than the mild ache you may feel in your knees.

a deeper problem. Typical symptoms include regularly forgetting things you really should remember, such as doctor's appointments or a weekly card game, frequently misplacing items and having difficulty following a conversation.

People with this condition are often aware that they're slipping, but possess the intelligence and social skills to cover mistakes so well that others may not notice. But this could be an early-warning sign of impending dementia and, like dementia, has a range of causes, some of which are reversible. Some people with MCI do go on to develop dementia but many don't. Elsewhere in the book, you'll find plenty of advice on memory techniques and aids to help symptoms, reducing their interference in your life.

● **When it's much more serious.** People who are described as having dementia there's evidence that a combination of proper medication, nutrition and a fitness programme, can help to mitigate the symptoms.

FOR MOST OF US, THE BEST IS YET TO COME

If the older brain is not quite as agile as it once was, it has just as much capacity as the young brain. Remember that although in timed tests of knowledge, younger adults do better than most older adults, if you take away the time factor, older adults do better. Plus, those lab tests of memory skill tend to ask subjects to study and spit back lists of words or numbers. That's a small part of the total cognitive picture.

NORMAL or NOT?

The majority of us worry about the state of our brains at one time or another. But most of the time, our cognitive slips are perfectly normal. The main problem is knowing whether you should laugh it off or see a doctor. Here's how to tell a routine brain hiccup from a matter of serious concern.

PROBABLY NORMAL	SEE A DOCTOR
You feel forgetful, but your family and friends don't notice it.	Your family and friends tell you that they are worried about your forgetfulness.
Sometimes you struggle to find the word you were looking for.	You often lose words and have to use substitutes or change the subject to avoid embarrassment.
You can come up with examples of times when you felt your forgetfulness was worrying.	You know that you've been forgetful, but you can't remember details – you forget what it was you forgot.
You enjoy seeing friends at your usual level. Socialising is fun and enjoyable.	You avoid social activities because you're afraid that you'll do something embarrassing.
You find it difficult to learn how to use new appliances or electronic devices.	You find it impossible to learn to use new appliances, and you even find it difficult to use the old ones.
You frequently lose your car keys.	You look at a key and can't remember how to use it.
You walk into a room and forget why you went there.	You forget how to find the kitchen in your own home.
You forget the name of a person you were just introduced to.	You forget the name of a family member.
You momentarily forget the name of a close friend.	You don't remember the person who says he or she is your friend.
You put the paper towels in the refrigerator and the milk in the cupboard and have a good laugh about it.	You frequently have no idea where things are supposed to go.
Mornings can be hectic, and you sometimes find it difficult to leave the house on time because you misplaced your belt or forgot to set the alarm clock.	People comment because you leave the house without showering or because your clothes are dishevelled.
You take a wrong turn on the way to your favourite food shop, or get momentarily lost in familiar territory.	You sometimes leave home and can't find your way back.
You forget to go to your dentist appointment.	You forget to go to your daughter's wedding.
If asked, you could give details about yesterday's dinner or your most recent phone call. It might take a while, but you can do it.	You have difficulty remembering recent events. Or you may not recall them at all.

Older adults do much better on tests of semantic knowledge, such as vocabulary tests or general knowledge, than they do on episodic or working memory tests.

Also, studies led by Professor Louise Phillips at the University of Aberdeen and Professor Matthias Kliegel at the University of Dresden, Germany, have revealed a curious paradox. In laboratory settings, young people generally outperform older people in tests of prospective memory – remembering to do things. But when tested in more naturalistic settings, such as their own homes, older adults actually do better than younger adults, especially when there is emotional or social importance attached to 'remembering to remember'.

Why this is so is not entirely clear, but it may in part be because a familiar environment supplies more of the cues used for prospective memory. Also, older people more often spontaneously use reminders, such as Post-it notes and diaries – just the kind of memory techniques that you'll learn about in this book – whereas younger people tend to rely totally on their memory, which may be better but is still fallible.

Scientists can't even come close to measuring the true intricacy – and deep reserves – of the older brain. Cognitive neuroscientists who study memory not only in the lab but also in everyday real-life settings know a great deal about what the older brain is capable of as well as where its limitations lie.

'As people get older, their life experience and well-honed skills make them capable of so much more than many of them imagine. The trick is to gather experience and skills throughout life to make it interesting no matter how old we are,' says Professor Logie.

● **Give yourself credit.** The first step in fighting brain decline is applauding the amazing potential you already possess. Another way to put it: you're probably in better shape than you think. In fact, sometimes, what feels like deterioration is actually something much more benign: mental laziness. We forget a name because we've just not made the effort to learn it.

In timed tests of knowledge, younger adults do better, but take away the time factor, and older adults win.

● **Take action.** The single key lesson is this: use it or lose it. Flex those mental muscles in order to preserve your powers of attention, comprehension and recall. So, the all-important second step in fighting brain decline is to decide consciously to do something about it. By reading this book, you've already begun.

● **Apply some grit and determination.** The third step: use a little elbow grease. This book aims to arm you with the most up-to-date advice on keeping your brain fit, capable and ready for action. In Part 2, use the Brain Fitness Programme, which includes specially designed exercises and strategies to increase your brainpower. In Part 3, you'll find ideas for lifestyle changes that will benefit your brain.

Yes, you're being asked to do some work, but this sort of work is more like play. It's time to get started.

YOUR BRAIN FITNESS PROGRAMME

part 2

INCREASE YOUR BRAIN POWER

in minutes a day

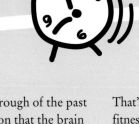

The big brain breakthrough of the past decade is confirmation that the brain can constantly change and adapt to meet new challenges. And by challenging it ourselves, we can actually encourage it to grow new brain cells and form new connections between those cells for faster, more efficient, more effective thinking.

In retrospect, it seems odd that scientists should find this surprising. Every other part of the body changes, including the bones, which seem rock solid but are constantly breaking themselves down and building themselves back up. The more you tax your bones with weight-bearing exercise, the stronger they are forced to grow. Likewise, the more you challenge your brain, the stronger it will become.

That's why this book includes a brain fitness programme. The exercises and strategies are designed to improve your performance in six main areas of cognitive function (see box, right). Try to do these and similar exercises and strategies for at least 20 minutes a day. You should feel more alert and 'with it' almost instantly once you give your brain a jolt of stimulation.

THE EVIDENCE

In 2003, the prestigious US *New England Journal of Medicine* printed an article with the title 'Use it or lose it', discussing the potential benefits of staying mentally active. It appeared after a 5 year study by researchers at the Albert Einstein College of Medicine of Yeshiva University in New York suggested that leisure activities

– including reading, playing board games, playing a musical instrument and dancing – might reduce the risk of developing dementia by more than half.

That seemed an amazing benefit for such enjoyable activities. To date there is not sufficient evidence to confirm that this is always the case, as genes also seem to play a role in whether or not people develop dementia in later life. But what is becoming increasingly evident is that keeping the brain active throughout life can help to compensate for the natural cognitive decline that occurs with age.

TRAINING HONES SKILLS

In 2006, the *Journal of the American Medical Association* published results of the study known as ACTIVE – Advanced Cognitive Training for Independent and Vital Elderly. People over the age of 65 were taught how to improve memory, reasoning and processing speed, then were evaluated immediately and five years later. After 10 short sessions, people who received the training not only did better in those areas than those who were not trained but also maintained their superior skills when they were retested five years

later. This shows that practising a skill can bring improvement at any time of life.

It may be, of course, that the shining examples of acute minds at an advanced age belong to people who have always enjoyed keeping their brains active. But this and other observational research does suggest that, with the right sort of stimulation – such as the tricks and strategies you'll find here – it is possible to combat some age-related problems, such as slower processing of new information and a slightly smaller capacity for storing short-term memories.

BEFORE YOU BEGIN

Look back at your scores in the quiz on pages 8-9 to help you to determine a personal brain-boosting strategy. From your answers and the 'Where should I start?' panel below, you can work out which of the six areas of cognitive function you should focus on the most.

These exercises should be the beginning of your brain training, not the end. Your advanced studies need to take place out in the world. Opportunities to expand your brain power are all around you; you just need to reach out and take them.

Where should I start?

In the quiz you took on pages 8-9, the questions addressed six areas of cognitive function. The more True answers you had in a particular category, the more help you need in that area. For easy reference, the following puzzles are colour-coded to address the same six areas – so you can choose which skills to practise first.

- ATTENTION AND FOCUS
- MEMORY
- PROCESSING SPEED
- VERBAL SKILLS
- NUMBER SKILLS
- REASONING SKILLS

IMPROVE YOUR ATTENTION

and focus

When was the last time you really lost yourself in a good book or became so enthralled with a project that hours flew by like minutes? It happens all the time in childhood but, as you get older, it can become much harder to focus intensely.

No one knows exactly why age tends to affect our ability to concentrate but one popular theory is that younger people have some sort of system that keeps irrelevant and extraneous information from interfering with attention.

Think of this system as mulch in a garden to keep down the weeds. A teenager has 'mulch' so thick that he or she can do maths homework with music blaring and occasionally stop to answer a text message. With age, though, the 'mulch' thins, allowing more and more distractions to creep in. When too many get through, they can affect how well we learn and remember, as well as how we perform certain tasks. Let's say you're driving along and spot some rubbish at the side of the road, which makes you wonder whether you took the refuse bag out of the kitchen, which reminds you that you need to pick up onions for dinner, which leads to thoughts of crying and eyes and your appointment with the optician next week. All of a sudden, your focus switches back to the road and you see that you've driven miles without realising it, and perhaps even missed your turning.

ATTENTION, PLEASE!

No one can pay attention to everything. Information blasts into your senses constantly. Every colour, object, sound, taste, odour or physical sensation is taken into the brain and processed. But most of these inputs are ignored, as they should be. It would be exhausting to be hypervigilant at every moment; there's no real need to remember what kind of bird just flew by your window. Instead, you choose what to pay attention to, like the email you were reading when the bird flew by. It's that information that you hold in your short-term memory.

As you get older, you tend to have less working memory (as short-term memory is also called). Unless you pay close attention, the information just doesn't stick as well as it used to. That's one reason why an older person might have trouble moving back and forth between one task and another. Let's say you're trying to read alternately from two chapters in a book. When you switch chapters, you may lose your place in the first chapter and struggle to reorient yourself, while a younger person with greater working memory would have less difficulty.

MORE ENERGY REQUIRED

Focus is closely linked to attention. If you think of attention as turning on a light in a dark room, focus is turning a laser beam on a specific object in the room. Focus is that intense level of attention that makes you feel as though you are burning memories into your brain. You lose some of that ability as you age, too. The small details simply vanish. If you read a passage in a book, you might remember the gist of it, but a younger person will be more likely to be able to recall exact sentences.

You don't lose your ability to focus entirely; it's just that it takes more energy and interest. What you gain is the ability to absorb a broader view of the world – a sum of the parts. Younger people tend to see the parts, but might miss how they fit into the bigger picture. The tips and exercises in this chapter are designed to help you improve both your attention and focus, so you can make it through *War and Peace* if you choose to, or at least a long newspaper feature. And the challenge of a new laptop, mobile phone or MP3 player should seem less daunting once you've finished here.

HAVE A GO

These exercises challenge your attention and focus, training your brain to concentrate. Regardless of how well you do or how quickly you complete each exercise, you win as you are practising a skill that will help you to absorb and recall information.

Read & remember ...

For this exercise, you'll need a pencil.

Below, you'll find a series of short articles. Read them carefully, trying to remember as much detail as possible. Then, without looking back at the article, answer the questions on the next page. You'll probably notice that it's easier to retain details when reading about topics with which you're already somewhat familiar. The same is true in real life.

● Read 1

Many people who enjoy solving crosswords have wondered how crosswords are made. Those who have tried to create a puzzle of their own, perhaps for a friend's birthday, were probably surprised at how difficult it was. No doubt they discovered that solving crosswords and making them up are two very different talents, each requiring its own set of skills. Yes, there is some overlap. You'll need a good vocabulary and a wide-ranging base of general knowledge to do both successfully. But the skill similarities pretty much end there.

Consider this analogy from the world of music. Playing the piano is very different from composing a symphony. There are, of course, people noted for excelling at both composition and performance – George Gershwin, Franz Liszt and Sergei Rachmaninov come to mind.

It's safe to say that solving crosswords is much easier than making them. And there's a special art involved in creating cryptic crosswords, which are very popular in Britain but, interestingly, much less common in the United States. Cryptic crosswords involve wordplay and solving a clue usually requires a degree of lateral thinking. Part of the clue is a straight definition but the rest includes coded language that a cryptic crossword enthusiast learns to unravel, for instance, 'about' may mean turning the letters of a word around.

And if you've ever wondered whether compilers of either type of crossword create the clues or the word diagram first, here's a hint: Try to make your own 3-by-3 crossword by writing the clues first; you'll quickly see the answer for yourself.

Now answer questions on page 68

Read 2

The Euro is the official currency of most of the member nations of the European Union. The nations that use the Euro exclusively form what's known as the Eurozone. Euro coins and banknotes entered circulation on January 1, 2002, as the national currency of 11 countries: Austria, Belgium, Finland, France, Germany, Ireland, Italy, Luxembourg, the Netherlands, Portugal and Spain. The Euro is managed and administered by the Frankfurt-based European Central Bank. The inspiration for the distinctive € symbol was the Greek letter Epsilon, a reference to the cradle of European civilisation.

The Euro is divided into 100 cents. Euro coins come in eight different denominations, ranging from 1 cent to 2 Euros, although by Finnish law, cash transactions are rounded to the nearest 5 cents, so that 1 cent and 2 cent coins aren't needed. There are seven Euro banknote denominations, from 5 to 500 (€5, €10, €20, €50, €100, €200, and €500). Each denomination has its own size and colour, in part to help visually impaired people to recognise them.

Now answer questions on page 68

Read 3

Have you ever watched a cartoon or children's programme where someone's cooked a soufflé and a tiny poke or a sudden loud noise makes it collapse?

Soufflés lend themselves to that sort of mockery because they're full of air. And 'soufflé', the past particle of the French verb 'souffler' (to blow) can sometimes mean 'blown up' or 'exploded'. Whether prepared as a savoury main dish or a sweet dessert, every soufflé is made from two basic components: a base of custard or a flavoured cream sauce, and egg whites beaten into a soft meringue. The base provides the flavour, while the egg whites provide the lift. Soufflés are traditionally served in flat-bottomed, round porcelain containers called ramekins.

If prepared correctly, your soufflé will be puffed up and fluffy when you take it out of the oven. But be sure to serve it quickly – soufflés generally fall within 5 to 10 minutes.

Now answer questions on page 68

Read & remember QUESTIONS

Read 1 Questions

1 Who is the first composer mentioned?

2 What type of crosswords are much more popular in Britain than America?

3 The two skills required both to solve and make general crosswords are a wide-ranging base of general knowledge and what else?

4 What might the word 'about' suggest in a cryptic crossword?

5 As implied by the passage, do crossword-writers create the clues or the word diagram first?

Read 2 Questions

1 What is the term for the group of European nations that uses the Euro?

2 In what year did the Euro enter circulation?

3 How many countries adopted it at the start?

4 How many different Euro banknote denominations are there?

5 What nation doesn't use the two smallest Euro coin denominations?

Read 3 Questions

1 What can 'soufflé' also mean in French?

2 What ingredient provides the lift in a soufflé?

3 What are soufflé containers called?

4 What form do the egg whites take when beaten?

5 How soon after being taken out of the oven will soufflés generally fall?

Check your answers by rereading the articles.

Smart **EVERYDAY STRATEGIES**

All of us get distracted and lose our focus now and then. If it happens to you a lot, get in the habit of using these strategies to help compensate.

❋ Take notes

Writing forces you to pay attention and also helps move the information from short-term memory into long-term memory. And, of course, it provides a solid record if you need it later on.

❋ Carry a pocket-size recorder

For years, patient advocates have been advising people to take a small cassette or digital recorder when they see a doctor. When people are nervous or under stress, they may not accurately or fully remember what was said in an office visit. The same strategy can help in everyday life. If you carry a recorder, you can use a voice-activation feature to capture important conversations or even personal memos to yourself. You can then review the recording any time you want to.

❋ Invest in a pair of noise-reducing headphones

Unlike earplugs, these gadgets reduce or eliminate ambient sound while slightly muffling distinct sounds. For example, if you wear them in the office, you'll eliminate the hum of machinery and background chatter, while being able to hear someone speaking to you or the sound of a telephone ringing.

❋ Control sensory distractions

Take charge of the controllable distractions around you by turning off the music, television, and radio. If you are cold, put on a sweater. If you are hungry, eat. If the air feels stagnant, open a window. The more comfortable you are, the better you'll be able to focus.

❋ Find a quiet corner

If you don't have total noise control, take yourself to another location. Libraries are often quiet, or at least quieter than a busy home.

❋ Boost concentration with caffeine

Researchers from the University of Arizona in Tucson discovered that people over the age 65 who felt that their attention was highest in the morning (as opposed to 'night owls' who concentrate best late at night) could improve their focus by drinking 350ml regular coffee. Decaffeinated coffee didn't work. And this trick only works if you are already a coffee-drinker. If not, the side effects of caffeine – that jittery buzz – will only disrupt your attention.

Name that shape ...

For this exercise, you'll need a pencil and a watch or clock with a second hand.

Below, you'll see a grid containing geometric shapes with the names of the shapes underneath. Your goal is to make sure that the shapes and names match, so that each shape has a correct name in the corresponding position on the grid. If you spot a mistake, circle the incorrect word and continue on.

Third word ('star') should be circled.

These exercises will be scored for accuracy. But time is also important, so work as quickly as possible. When you have completed each one, write down the amount of time you needed to finish in the space provided at the bottom. Score the exercise before moving on to the next one. When you are ready, set the timer and begin.

For example:

SQUARE   STAR   STAR   SQUARE

● Shape card 1

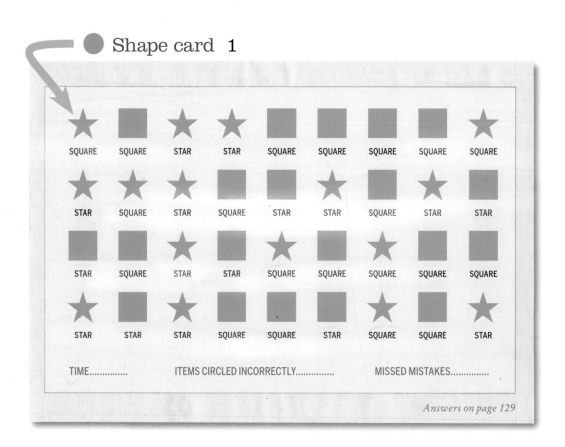

SQUARE	SQUARE	STAR	STAR	SQUARE	SQUARE	SQUARE	SQUARE	SQUARE
STAR	SQUARE	STAR	SQUARE	STAR	STAR	SQUARE	STAR	STAR
STAR	SQUARE	STAR	STAR	SQUARE	SQUARE	SQUARE	SQUARE	SQUARE
STAR	STAR	STAR	SQUARE	SQUARE	STAR	SQUARE	SQUARE	STAR

TIME.............   ITEMS CIRCLED INCORRECTLY...............   MISSED MISTAKES...............

Answers on page 129

Shape card 2

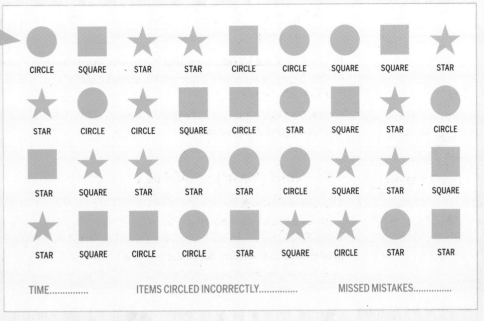

CIRCLE	SQUARE	STAR	STAR	CIRCLE	CIRCLE	SQUARE	SQUARE	STAR
STAR	CIRCLE	CIRCLE	SQUARE	CIRCLE	STAR	SQUARE	STAR	CIRCLE
STAR	SQUARE	STAR	STAR	STAR	CIRCLE	SQUARE	STAR	SQUARE
STAR	SQUARE	CIRCLE	CIRCLE	STAR	SQUARE	CIRCLE	STAR	STAR

TIME..............   ITEMS CIRCLED INCORRECTLY..............   MISSED MISTAKES..............

Answers on page 129

Shape card 3

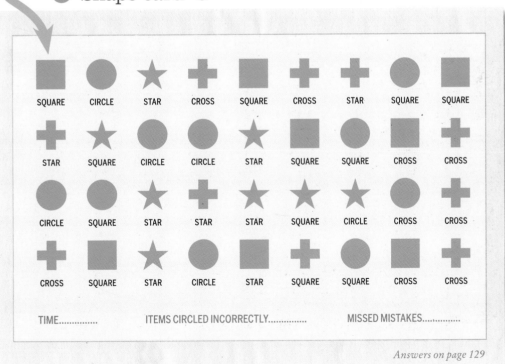

SQUARE	CIRCLE	STAR	CROSS	SQUARE	CROSS	STAR	SQUARE	SQUARE
STAR	SQUARE	CIRCLE	CIRCLE	STAR	SQUARE	SQUARE	CROSS	CROSS
CIRCLE	SQUARE	STAR	STAR	STAR	SQUARE	CIRCLE	CROSS	CROSS
CROSS	SQUARE	STAR	CIRCLE	STAR	SQUARE	SQUARE	CROSS	CROSS

TIME..............   ITEMS CIRCLED INCORRECTLY..............   MISSED MISTAKES..............

Answers on page 129

Shape card 4

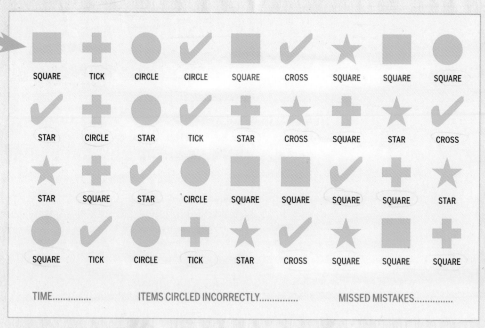

SQUARE	TICK	CIRCLE	CIRCLE	SQUARE	CROSS	SQUARE	SQUARE	SQUARE
STAR	CIRCLE	STAR	TICK	STAR	CROSS	SQUARE	STAR	CROSS
STAR	SQUARE	STAR	CIRCLE	SQUARE	SQUARE	SQUARE	SQUARE	STAR
SQUARE	TICK	CIRCLE	TICK	STAR	CROSS	SQUARE	SQUARE	SQUARE

TIME...............   ITEMS CIRCLED INCORRECTLY..............   MISSED MISTAKES...............

Answers on page 129

Shape card 5

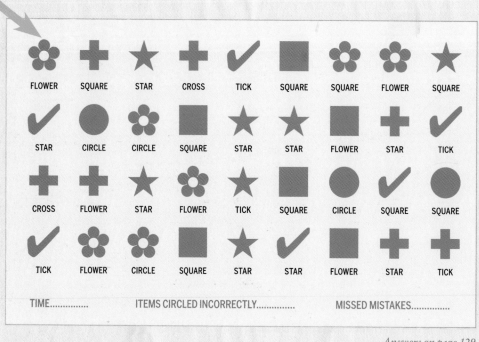

FLOWER	SQUARE	STAR	CROSS	TICK	SQUARE	SQUARE	FLOWER	SQUARE
STAR	CIRCLE	CIRCLE	SQUARE	STAR	STAR	FLOWER	STAR	TICK
CROSS	FLOWER	STAR	FLOWER	TICK	SQUARE	CIRCLE	SQUARE	SQUARE
TICK	FLOWER	CIRCLE	SQUARE	STAR	STAR	FLOWER	STAR	TICK

TIME...............   ITEMS CIRCLED INCORRECTLY..............   MISSED MISTAKES...............

Answers on page 129

Odd one out …

For this exercise, you'll need a pencil.

Below, you'll see what looks like a number of identical items. Only one item in the group is different from the others. Find and circle that item. This is not a timed exercise.

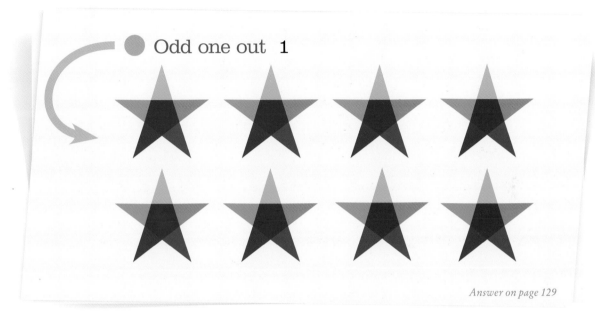

Odd one out 1

Answer on page 129

Odd one out 2

Answer on page 129

Odd one out 3

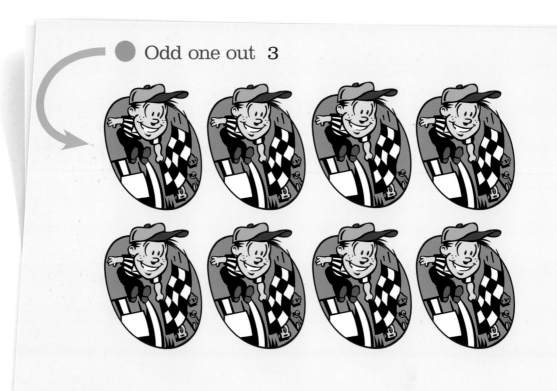

Odd one out 4

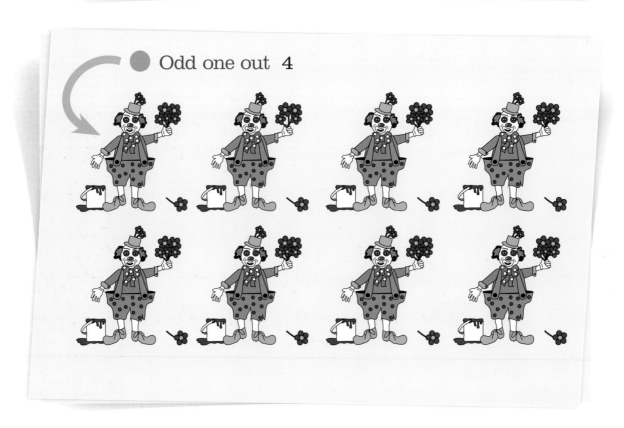

Odd one out 5

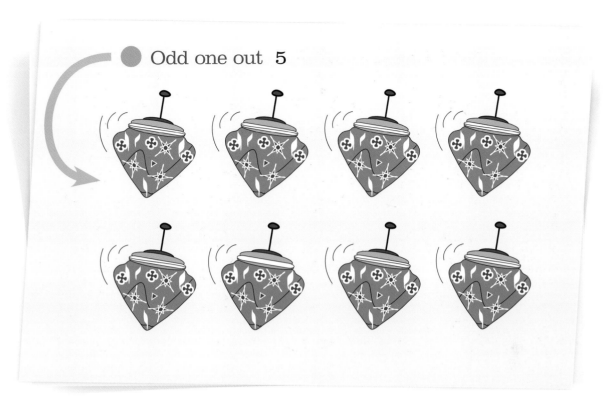

Odd one out 6

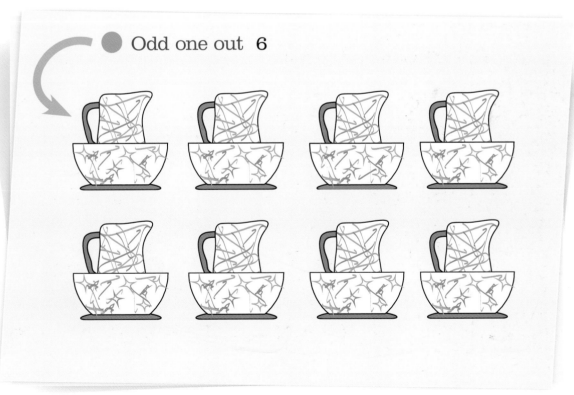

Answers on page 129

Spot the difference ...

For this exercise, you'll need a pencil.

The picture pairs here are nearly identical, but not quite. Find the specified number of differences and circle them. This is not a timed exercise.

 Picture 1

There are three differences. Can you see them?

Answers on page 130

Picture 2

Can you identify the four differences?

Answers on page 130

Picture 3

There are five differences. Can you see them?

Answers on page 130

Picture 4

Can you spot the six differences?

Answers on page 130

Improve your MEMORY

When people talk about their memory getting worse, they usually mean those aspects of memory that allow them to function in the world – remembering appointments, the location of car keys, items on a to-do list, work deadlines, even basic facts.

We can run into real trouble when our memory lets us down, especially when it comes to 'remembering' future events. Imagine if you forgot to pay your house insurance premium. That slip could cost thousands of pounds if the house were flooded or caught fire. Luckily, most memory slips are less serious.

KEEPING TRACK

Keys, sunglasses, mobile phone, car in a multi-storey car park – if you haven't 'lost' one of these items in the past month, then you're doing well in the memory department. Misplacing objects is normal at any age, especially when you're under stress. You lose track of items because the brain is so darned efficient. When you perform routine tasks, your body goes on automatic pilot. Let's say that every day, you come home and drop the keys in the same general location. But if something interrupts you – perhaps the phone is ringing as you open the door – then your brain is preoccupied with the new task. Your automatic pilot disengages, you drop the keys somewhere new, and later you have to search to find them.

RECALLING THE PAST

The ability to retrieve memories of past events declines with age. Recognition remains strong, but recall weakens. This is a fine but important distinction. Recall is the ability to pull up a memory simply by thinking about it. Recognition is the ability to remember once prompted with a cue. For example, if you were asked to name all the places to which you have ever travelled, your list would probably be incomplete. But if you were asked if you had ever been to Egypt, you could answer definitively yes or no.

If you want to remember on your own, you need to provide your own cues. That's one reason people buy souvenirs – to remind them of the details of a trip. For everyday purposes, we can use our imaginations instead.

'REMEMBERING' THE FUTURE

The most annoying of all memory problems involves prospective memory – the need to recall things that have yet to happen, such as an appointment or an anniversary. When this type of memory fails, we may forget to take medication, call at the supermarket for milk, or return a DVD on time. Experts who specialise in this aspect of memory call this 'remembering to remember'.

As far as the brain is concerned, this is much more difficult to pull off than other types of remembering, thanks to the gap in time between intending to do something and actually doing it.

Though everyone has prospective memory failures, some research has shown that these types of slips tend to become more common as we get older. One recent UK study of nearly 320,000 people, aged between 8 and 50 years, suggests that 'remembering to remember' starts to decline in early adulthood and throughout life. However, age is not the only determining factor. Stress, lack of sleep and the side effects of medication have all been shown to influence the forgetfulness factor.

SMART EVERYDAY STRATEGIES

No one's memory is perfect. Yours doesn't have to be either. But it's easy enough not to lose your car keys or forget another appointment simply by using some commonsense strategies. Save your brain power for other things.

Establish routines. Boring as it seems, it really is easier to find things if you always put them in the same place. Put up a hook somewhere to hang your car keys and create a special folder for unpaid bills, for instance. Find repositories for all the things you tend to misplace.

If you have to put an item in an unfamiliar place, say what you are doing out loud, as in, 'I am putting my sunglasses on the table by the door'. All sensory channels create their own neural links to the information. By letting your ears register the information, you increase your chances of remembering it later.

MEMORY CUES

Make full use of Post-it notes. Keep a pad of them in every room and stick a reminder where you are likely to see it. Concerned that you might forget to call a friend? Put a note on the phone and another in a spot that you are likely to notice during the day, such as on the television or on your computer keyboard.

Let technology remember for you. Mobile phones, Blackberries and other electronic devices have calendars you can set to remind you of what you need to do during the day. Some types of software have a 'notes' function you can program to remind you of what you need to do during the day.

Once you have learnt how to use these systems, you'll wonder how you ever got along without them. And yes, almost anyone can learn to use them. Researchers have taught people with significant memory problems – those with brain injuries and mild to moderate Alzheimer's disease – to use such devices successfully. Just make sure you keep a back-up, such as a wall calendar, day planner, or external hard drive.

Use checklists. People make lists for a reason: they work. Tick off each to-do item as you complete it. The more you have, the more likely you are to refer to it again and again, each time reinforcing your memory of the tasks there.

Plant a visual reminder. If you need to remember to take an umbrella, hang it on the door handle. Visual reminders can even help you to accomplish goals. For example, if you decide you want to begin a healthy diet tomorrow, put the porridge oats on the worktop the night before.

You can also use imaginary cues when planting a visual clue is impossible. If you go to a museum and have to check in a bag or briefcase, how can you remember to collect it? By using your imagination. Robert Logie, professor of human cognitive neuroscience at Edinburgh University suggests this: when you first realise that you will need to use prospective memory, look for physical landmarks to trigger it.

It could be a distinctive door or a statue or other permanent fixture. Then, imagine your item and the landmark together. In the museum example, you can imagine a briefcase blocking the doorway. In studies, these imaginary cues proved to be as effective as external cues. Imaginary cues work best when you are in an unfamiliar location or situation and therefore less likely to go on autopilot.

DON'T PROCRASTINATE

Do it now, not later. Although this won't work in all situations, the best way to remember to do something is to do it while you're thinking about it. Instead of telling yourself to remember to make a phone call or pay a bill, why not do it immediately? Too often it's procrastination that makes us forget.

HAVE A GO

You must remember this...

For this exercise, you'll need a timer.

Set the timer for 5 minutes. Read one of the questions, then close your eyes and remember all the details you can. Try to think on all sensory fronts: sight, sound, smell, taste and touch. Don't rush the process; take the full 5 minutes. After the timer goes off, open your eyes. Did you remember more than you thought you would?

- How did you celebrate your 13th birthday?
- How did you get to school in your last year at primary school?
- What do you remember about your best friend's wedding?
- What do you remember about your most recent holiday?
- Where and with whom was your first kiss?
- What was the best birthday present you ever got?
- What do you remember most about your grandparents?
- How did you spend summers as a child?
- Which dance steps or music groups were popular when you were in secondary school?
- What do you remember about the first job you ever held?
- What books have you read in the past year?
- What films have you seen in the past year?
- How did you and your friends spend your time after school when you were 10?
- What was your first pet?
- What was your most intimidating moment?
- When did you get your first bicycle?
- What was your favourite book as a child?
- Who was your favourite primary-school teacher?
- What did the first house you lived in look like?
- Who was your first love?

Picture recall ...

For this exercise, you'll need a pencil and a timer.

Set the timer for 2 minutes and study the picture below. After 2 minutes, turn the page. There you'll find a picture that is identical to this one except for a few details. Repeat for the other two pictures on page 85.

● Observe 1

Observe 2

Observe 3

Recall 1

Without looking back, circle the details that have changed. How many can you identify?

Answers on page 131

Recall 2

Recall 3

Answers on page 131

Concentration ...

For this exercise, you'll need a pencil and a timer.

Set the timer for 1 minute and study the grid below. After a minute, turn the page. There you'll find a blank grid and two rows of objects. Match the objects to their proper locations on the grid. Repeat the exercise with all the following grids.

● Concentration 1

Concentration 2

● Recall 1

Each picture is labelled with a letter. Try to recall where each picture was located on the grid, then write the letter associated with the picture in the proper place on the grid. Do the same for 'Recall 2' (opposite).

A B C D E

F G H I

To check your answers, turn back to page 88

Recall 2

To check your answers, turn back to page 89

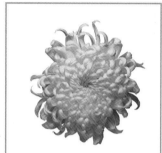

Concentration 4

Recall 3

A B C D E

F G H I

To check your answers, turn back to page 92

Recall 4

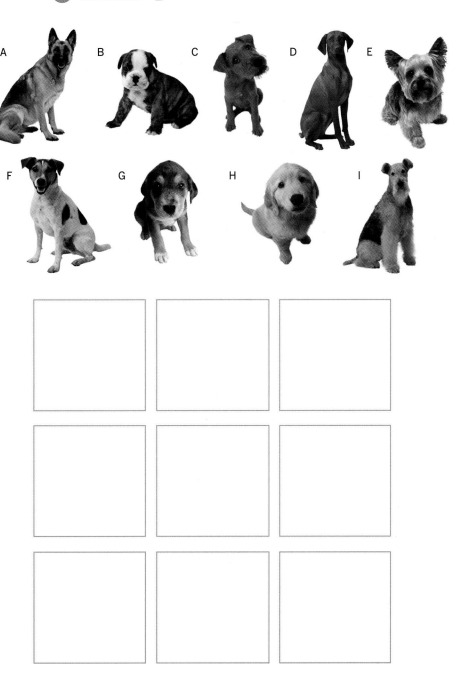

A   B   C   D   E

F   G   H   I

To check your answers, turn back to page 93

Scents and sensibility ...

For this exercise, you'll need a pencil and a timer.

Certain scents have the amazing ability to transport you back to a particular time, place, or moment in your life. The olfactory bulb, the area of the brain that perceives smells, is part of the brain's limbic system, which plays a major role in long-term memory, especially emotional memories.

 ## Scent memories 1

Set the timer for 5 minutes. Look at the list below and choose one of the scents. If you happen to have access to the scent, take a good sniff. Then, sit down without any distractions and imagine the smell as best you can. Let your mind recall every detail of the memories it evokes. Don't rush the process; take the full 5 minutes. Later, come back and do this exercise with other scents from the list.

cinnamon	old books
warm apple pie	wood smoke
hot chocolate	hay
freshly sharpened lead pencil	tobacco
fresh pine (or a pine-scented candle)	surgical spirit
roses	aftershave
cigars	nutmeg
wet dog	shoe polish
floral perfume	baking bread
baby powder	burning leaves
freshly mown grass	ripe Camembert
damp earth after a rainstorm	strawberry lip gloss
manure	lake water
homemade chicken soup	chlorine
mulled wine	

● Scent memories 2

Think of a scent that has special meaning for you. Maybe it's the perfume your mother wore on special occasions, a former boyfriend's aftershave, bread baking in your grandmother's kitchen, a lilac tree from your childhood garden, a leather chair from your father's study, the smell of wood and sawdust from your uncle's workshop, or sausages frying over a campfire. The possibilities are endless. For each scent you think of, write down the memory you associate with it.

SCENT ....

MEMORY ....

....

....

....

SCENT ....

MEMORY ....

....

....

....

SCENT ....

MEMORY ....

....

....

....

SCENT ....

MEMORY ....

....

....

....

Improve your *PROCESSING SPEED*

Have you watched a young child in action lately? **They don't walk; they run.** They don't sit; they fidget. As we get older, our bodies slow down. The same goes for our brains. We can learn and remember almost as well as we used to, but it might take our brains a bit longer.

The brain tends to operate more slowly with age because we naturally produce fewer neurotransmitters, the all-important brain chemicals that carry information across the gaps between brain cells. We also lose some of our white matter, the fatty substance that insulates the brain's high-speed information 'cables' (bundles of nerve fibres, really) that enable faster transmission of electrical signals from one part of the brain to another.

Lagging speed can affect our ability to understand a fast-moving scene in a movie, count change at the supermarket check-out, balance our accounts, or react to a car swerving in front of us on the highway. It can even affect how 'fast' the brain hears. Sounds that enter the ear take an extra moment or two to be registered and translated in the brain. Many older people are sent for hearing tests by family members who are later confused when the tests show normal hearing. The delay between hearing and responding is often interpreted as a hearing problem, when it is actually just a natural, if frustrating, slowdown in the brain.

That is also the reason why new memories do not form as quickly or as completely as they once did. But if we can't quite attain the thinking speed of our youth, there is no need for the mental equivalent of shuffling. Like a sprinter training for the Olympics, we can train our brains to go faster.

Smart **EVERYDAY STRATEGIES**

While you're using the exercises in this book to help increase your processing speed, also consider these strategies.

❋ Be deliberate and calm

As with all mental processes, speed suffers when you are stressed. If you find yourself feeling pressured by your own or others' expectations, take a deep breath, relax and remind yourself that you deserve to take as much time as you need.

❋ Practise

Everything you do, you can do faster with practice. The general reaction to doing poorly at tasks is to give up trying, but if speed is your problem, avoidance of the task will only make it worse. Work at small projects by practising them again and again, the way you would practise if you were learning to play a musical instrument, and soon your brain will find the 'notes' in no time.

❋ Check out computer games

The same computer games your children and grandchildren play can help improve your ability to see, process and react to fast-moving objects. You can also train your brain using video games designed specifically to improve cognitive abilities, including processing speed (see 'Can playing computer games make you cleverer?' on page 100). These can be played on a home computer or video game system. These may not necessarily speed up other mental processes, but there is some satisfaction in keeping up (if you can) with the digital skills of the young.

CAN PLAYING *computer games* MAKE YOU CLEVERER?

With so many baby boomers living in fear of brain deterioration, it's no wonder that computer games designed to improve brain fitness are on the market. There's Nintendo's Brain Age, Posit Science's Brain Fitness, and CogniFit's MindFit, to name a few, plus web-based programmes such as www.lumosity.com or UK sites such as www.braintrainingpuzzle.co.uk/. Do they work? The answer is yes and no – depending on your goals, how hard you are willing to work (or, in this case, play), and which software you use.

Imagine a teenager who wants to improve his overall athletic ability. What should he do? He could run on a track to improve his speed and endurance, but that won't help his basketball skills. He could spend weeks perfecting his dribbling technique, but that won't help his ability to score a basket. And none of that training will help his golf game.

VARIETY IS KEY

It's the same with brain training. Cognitive abilities come in many distinct types. The best programmes work on several types, including processing speed, visual acuity, listening, concentration and focus, reasoning, spatial orientation and memory. These encourage general brain improvement, as opposed to what might be called the Sudoku effect – if you do Sudoku puzzles day and night, you can become fast at filling squares with numbers, but won't get any better at counting change at the supermarket.

Detractors say there is no proof that any of the games really help improve mental function and that the business is overwhelming the science. But practising certain skills is undoubtedly beneficial. For instance, Posit Science tested its eight-week programme on older adults (aged 60 to 97) and claims that memory improved significantly, even months later. Larger studies are underway at most of the serious brain fitness companies to determine if and how these games might prevent or delay age-related memory problems or even dementia.

Bottom line: the games may help and can't hurt anything but your wallet. Many people enjoy them, but, you don't have to buy computer games to keep your mind active.

'Everything you do helps in one way or another,' says memory expert Robert Logie, professor of human cognitive neuroscience at Edinburgh University. 'Playing an instrument, joining a choir or a special interest club, taking an evening class or learning a language are stimulating and also offer social benefits.'

Buy games for fun, he adds, but don't neglect the rest of the world; there are plenty of fascinating non-digital ways to challenge your mind.

If our reaction time slows, the world can pass us by. We become frustrated, and it's not difficult to feel that others are annoyed with us as well. These exercises were designed to improve the brain's processing speed. Do them every day, at least once a day.

HAVE A GO

Speed sorting ... Repeat three times a day, if possible.

For this exercise, you'll need a pen, paper, a watch or clock with a second hand and a pack of playing cards.

● Speed sort 1

● **PREPARE** Shuffle the deck well and place it face down in front of you.

● **BEGIN** Note the time when you begin. Pick up the deck and sort the cards into four piles by suit. Do this as quickly as you can. When you finish sorting, look at the clock and note the time.

● **FINISH** Write down how long it took you to complete the exercise – and try to beat your time next time. Then, for your own information, look through the piles to see how accurate you were.

TIME...............

NUMBER OF MISTAKES...............

● Speed sort 2

ONE STEP HARDER

Note the time you begin. Quickly separate the deck into piles by suit, then take each pile and order the cards by number, with aces low and picture cards in this order: Jacks, Queens, Kings. Do not record your time until both phases of the exercise are complete.

TIME............... NUMBER OF MISTAKES...............

● Speed sort 3

TWO STEPS HARDER

Note the time you begin. Separate the deck into six piles – aces in one pile, picture cards in a second pile and four piles of numbered cards by suit. Do not record your time until all phases of the exercise are complete.

 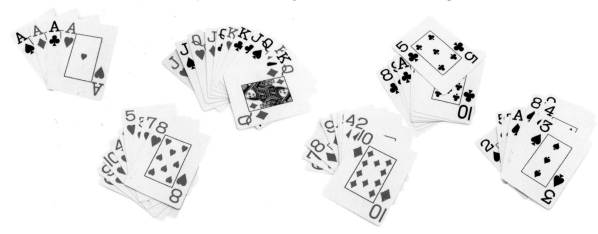

TIME............... NUMBER OF MISTAKES...............

Letter search ...

For this exercise, you'll need a pencil, paper and a watch or clock with a second hand.

● Letter search 1

In the grid below, find all appearances of the letter R, both capital and lower-case, any colour. When you are ready, set the stopwatch or note the time. Circle every letter R. Then go back and count how many appear in capital and how many in lower-case. Finally, count how many Rs appear in red. Note how long it took you, and see if you can beat your time in subsequent exercises.

K	a	N	M	r	r	N	c	N	m	n	k	A	r	X	c	X	m	x	r	N	a
k	R	n	n	r	k	r	X	B	k	k	M	z	N	r	n	k	r	X	N	Z	N
a	x	m	Z	r	R	r	K	Z	N	X	k	R	X	n	k	k	n	R	a	k	X
x	r	x	n	Z	k	m	X	R	r	Z	c	m	x	Z	r	Z	m	X	Z	r	R
m	Z	c	Z	N	a	Z	n	Z	R	m	N	r	R	M	z	A	Z	m	c	k	R
R	m	z	n	X	r	Z	m	N	K	z	x	N	a	z	R	z	M	r	z	X	r
X	z	N	k	m	M	c	z	Z	r	c	X	R	N	n	z	K	R	a	K	k	n
c	m	z	R	z	k	c	M	N	Z	x	m	z	B	a	x	X	M	R	X	m	m
x	X	N	z	m	r	R	x	A	X	n	z	m	Z	X	N	z	M	n	X	a	X
n	X	A	k	r	n	m	x	R	a	X	R	R	r	m	c	R	n	B	a	k	z
k	x	z	M	Z	k	N	z	m	R	N	X	a	k	r	R	x	r	k	X	r	X
B	Z	r	X	r	K	a	Z	B	z	R	z	N	A	k	M	x	X	c	R	n	A
r	X	n	x	a	R	M	k	k	Z	x	r	X	k	a	c	K	x	R	n	R	z
c	x	z	N	R	x	c	M	m	R	n	z	B	M	x	R	z	n	R	z	x	M
N	R	r	R	z	r	R	n	Z	R	n	m	R	A	a	X	X	r	m	R	n	Z
R	z	R	z	N	z	B	x	R	R	r	Z	x	R	n	X	a	z	m	R	x	n

Time................

Number of capital Rs................

Number of Rs in lower case................

Number of Rs in red................

Answers on page 132

Letter search 2

In the grid below, find all appearances of the letter N, both capital and lower-case, any colour. When you are ready, set the stopwatch or note the time. Circle every letter N. Then go back and count how many appear in capital and how many in lower-case. Finally, count how many Ns appear in blue. Note how long it took you.

```
K a N M r r N c N m n k A r X c X m x r N a
k R n n r k r X B k k M z N r n k r X N Z N
a x m Z r R r K Z N X k R X n k k n R a k X
x r x n Z k m X R r Z c m x Z r Z m X Z r R
m Z c Z N a Z n Z R m N r R M z A Z m c k R
R m z n X r Z m N K z x N a z R z M r z X r
X z N k m M c z Z r c X R N n z K R a K k n
c m z R z k c M N Z x m z B a x X M R X m m
x X N z m r R x A X n z m Z X N z M n X a X
n X A k r n m x R a X R R r m c R n B a k z
k x z M Z k N z m R N X a k r R x r k X r X
B Z r X r K a Z B z R z N A K M x X c R n A
r X n x a R M k k Z x r X k a c K x R n R z
c x z N R x c M m R n z B M X R z n R z x M
N R r R z r R n Z R n m R A a X X r m R n Z
R z R z N z B x R R r Z x R n X a z m R x n
c x z N R x c M m R n z B M X R z n R z x M
n x z M Z k N z m R N X a k r R x r k X r X
R m z n X r Z m N K z x N a z R z M r z X r
```

Time...............   Number of capital Ns...............

Number of Ns in lower case...............   Number of Ns in blue...............

Answers on page 132

Letter search 3

In the grid below, find all appearances of the letter K, both capital and lower-case, any colour. When you are ready, set the stopwatch or note the time. Circle every letter K. Then go back and count how many appear in capital and how many in lower-case. Finally, count how many Ks appear in green. Note how long it took you.

K	a	N	M	r	r	N	c	N	m	n	k	A	r	X	c	X	m	x	r	N	a
k	R	n	n	r	k	r	X	B	k	k	M	z	N	r	n	k	r	X	N	Z	N
a	x	m	Z	r	R	r	K	Z	N	X	k	R	X	n	k	k	n	R	a	k	X
x	r	x	n	Z	k	m	X	R	r	Z	c	m	x	Z	r	Z	m	X	Z	r	R
m	Z	c	Z	N	a	Z	n	Z	R	m	N	r	R	M	z	A	Z	m	c	k	R
R	m	z	n	X	r	Z	M	m	N	K	z	x	N	a	z	R	z	M	r	z	X	r
X	z	N	k	m	M	c	z	Z	r	c	X	R	N	n	z	K	R	a	K	K	n
c	m	z	R	z	k	c	M	N	Z	x	m	z	B	a	x	X	M	R	X	m	m
x	X	N	z	m	r	R	x	A	X	n	z	m	Z	X	N	z	M	n	X	a	X
n	X	A	k	r	n	m	x	R	a	X	R	R	r	m	c	R	n	B	a	k	z
k	x	z	M	Z	k	N	z	m	R	N	X	a	k	r	R	x	r	k	X	r	X
B	Z	r	X	r	K	a	Z	B	z	R	z	N	A	K	M	x	X	c	R	n	A
r	X	n	x	a	R	M	k	k	Z	x	r	X	k	a	c	K	x	R	n	R	z
c	x	z	N	R	x	c	M	m	R	n	z	B	M	x	R	z	n	R	z	x	M
N	R	r	R	z	r	R	n	Z	R	n	m	R	A	a	X	X	r	m	R	n	Z
R	z	R	z	N	z	B	x	R	R	r	Z	x	R	n	X	a	z	m	R	x	n
k	R	n	n	r	k	r	X	B	k	k	M	z	N	r	n	k	r	X	N	Z	N
B	Z	r	X	k	K	a	Z	B	z	K	z	N	A	k	M	x	X	c	R	n	A
q	X	N	z	m	r	R	x	A	X	n	z	w	Z	X	K	z	p	n	X	a	Z

Time...............   Number of capital Ks...............

Number of Ks in lower case...............   Number of Ks in green...............   *Answers on page 132*

The ability to communicate with others is perhaps the single most valuable skill a person can have because it gives voice to the self. In prisons, solitary confinement – separating an individual from nearly all human contact – has been known to unhinge people from their psychological moorings and drive them crazy.

Improve your VERBAL SKILLS

Most of us will never experience solitary confinement, of course, but even small reductions in our ability to communicate and express ourselves can be distressing. When we are speaking and suddenly forget a word or a name, for instance, we feel as if our brains are betraying us.

The tip-of-the-tongue phenomenon, in which the word or fact we want feels close by but just out of reach, is universal. The information is right there, encoded in nerve cell pathways in our brains; we just can't always access it when we want to, especially as we get older.

You don't have to feel backed into a verbal corner. The research clearly shows that people who practise mental tricks to help them remember – known as mnemonic strategies – have an easier time recalling words, names and facts than people who wing it and hope for the best. You can improve simply by applying one of the techniques outlined here. Psychologists used to think that there was a single best mnemonic, but new theories suggest that any mnemonic technique is helpful. Read through them and try the one that fits your personal thinking style, or use more than one to meet different needs.

Smart EVERYDAY STRATEGIES

While you're working on your word skills with the exercises in this chapter, also learn and practise the following strategies, which will help to ensure that you can access the words you need, when you need them.

❋ Make up a story

For lists of words you want to remember short-term, such as a grocery list or a to-do list, experts recommend making up a story that links the words. The story should be as visual as possible (otherwise you're just creating words to remember other words) and as silly or ridiculous as you can imagine.

For example, let's say you have three words to remember – lamp, strawberries, car. You could imagine turning on a lamp outdoors and finding strawberries growing inside the car and overflowing out the windows. The more imaginative or elaborate your mental pictures, the better your chances of remembering the items.

❋ Group words together

For long lists of words that don't have to be memorised in order, group similar words together. You decide which categories to use. If you have a grocery list, you can group the items by location in the store, by food group, by size, by price or by where you will store the items when you get home.

❋ Listen for the name

When you meet someone for the first time and want to remember his or her name, the first step is to listen! Most people are so focused on making a good impression that they forget to pay attention to the person they are meeting.

Focus on hearing the person's name. Immediately repeat the name ('Nice to meet you, Frank'), and use it again when addressing the person in conversation. This is often a problem in British culture, where it can seem a little odd and rather impolite to keep repeating a person's name in this way. Yet, this is a shame because saying it only once or not at all almost guarantees that the name will be forgotten.

❋ Let a name tell a story

When you hear the name, think about how the name sounds and what images it evokes. For example, if you meet Marina Taylor, you can easily visualise a marina full of boats and a tailor sitting on the dock mending sails. You can take the exercise a step further to help you recall this person, and their name, in the future. If Marina is a redhead, let every boat in the marina be painted red. It will be almost impossible to forget her name after such an elaborate visual image.

Not all names can be so easily translated into images. In those cases, use whatever associations come to mind. For example, if you meet Ted Sutton, who is balding, you might remember that you have a cousin or another friend named Ted who is also balding. And that your cousin was married to a woman who used to live in the south London borough of Sutton. So you can imagine your bald cousin Ted sitting in the middle of a south London street.

❋ Sound out difficult names

The first time you meet Wojciech Cieszko, you will probably have a tough time coming up with a story that fits his name. In such a case, ask him to repeat his name slowly. As he does, sound it out in your head and imagine writing the phonetic spelling out on a slip of paper. Now, mentally staple the paper to a mental snapshot of the person.

HAVE A GO

Of all the memory problems people struggle with, weakened verbal skills may annoy us most because we have to use them every day. The exercises below will help to keep those skills up to scratch – and may prevent further erosion. But first, an exercise to test one of the 'everyday strategies' outlined on page 107.

For this exercise you'll need a pencil and a blank sheet of paper

● Memory jogger

Here's a list of words. Look at it for a minute, then turn over the book and write down as many as you can remember:

oranges
currants
yoghurt
bread
cheese
breakfast cereal
ham
chicken
marmalade
deodorant
pet food
light bulbs

Now look at this new list:

butter
bacon
flour
jam
apples
biscuits
orange juice
toothpaste
kitchen roll
foil
detergent
ice cream

This time, make up a story involving all the items, in any order. For instance, you might want to think of items on the list as cartoon characters in a children's story. Imagine a block of butter as Mrs Butter who sets off for some adventures that involve the strong smelling Mr Bacon who has just been covered in Flour by local prankster Jam Pot. This also makes the process of making up stories quite fun. Or you might prefer to generate something more logical, perhaps weaving the items into an account of everyday living, starring you. The mental images you conjure up as you compose your story will help the memory process.

Try making up your own story, using the list of words, then turn the book over and write down as many as you can remember. How did you do?

Irregular words

For this exercise, you'll need a pencil.

Below are groups of words. Within each group, one of the words does not fit in the same category as the others or differs in another specific way. Circle the irregular word.

1 broccoli, carrots, spinach, peas
2 brick, bubble, football, globe
3 eagle, sparrow, ostrich, blackbird
4 tennis, ping-pong, rugby, volleyball
5 antagonise, anger, inspire, infuriate
6 Braille, Morse code, dominoes, zebras
7 duck, badger, camel, hog
8 tree, ball, watch, sock
9 plant, car, money, cash
10 television, radio, play, film

Link-up

For this exercise, you'll need a pencil.

Below is a series of analogies. It's up to you to fill in the blanks. We've helped by providing the correct number of spaces needed.

1 DOWNPOUR is to RAIN as BLIZZARD is to: ___ ___ ___ ___
2 POUND is to PENNY as CENTURY is to: ___ ___ ___ ___
3 RECIPES is to COOKBOOK as MAPS is to: ___ ___ ___ ___ ___
4 CRICKET is to BAT as TENNIS is to: ___ ___ ___ ___ ___ ___
5 BLUE is to SAPPHIRE as RED is to: ___ ___ ___ ___
6 LION is to ROAR as BEE is to: ___ ___ ___ ___
7 HEN is to COCKEREL as FILLY is to: ___ ___ ___ ___
8 MOON is to CRATER as PAVEMENT is to: ___ ___ ___ ___ ___ ___ ___
9 SPIDER is to CRAWL as SNAKE is to: ___ ___ ___ ___ ___ ___ ___
10 BOILED SWEET is to SUGAR as TYRE is to: ___ ___ ___ ___ ___ ___

Answers on page 132

Circle-grams

Try to find the word formed by the letters.
Hint: The trick is figuring out where to start.

1

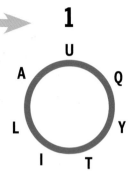

U A Q L Y I T

2

L I A Z E E R

3

R E V S E E D

4

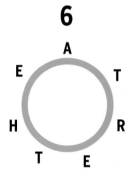

T P S I I A N

5

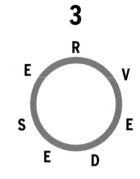

H E C E S S E

6

A E T H R T E

7

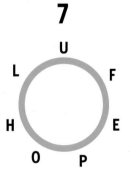

U L F H E O P

8

M I O N S O U

9

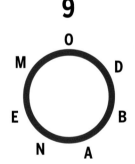

O M D E B N A

Answers on page 132

Opposites attract 1

Match each word with its antonym by writing its number next to each letter.

1	elated	.... A	ally
2	inspired	.... B	support
3	lazy	 C	beneficial
4	obscure	.... D	affirm
5	adversary	.... E	dejected
6	pernicious	.... F	industrious
7	oppose	.... G	mean-spirited
8	deny	.... H	ignore
9	address	 I	evident
10	affable	.... J	unmotivated

Opposites attract 2

1	futile	.... A	yield
2	penitent	.... B	disparaging
3	courage	 C	ungainly
4	agreeable	.... D	unpleasant
5	defy	.... E	remorseless
6	incessant	.... F	loquacious
7	taciturn	.... G	useful
8	careless	.... H	cowardice
9	elegant	 I	thoughtful
10	fawning	.... J	intermittent

Matching pairs 1

Match each word to its synonym by writing a number next to each letter.

1	settle	.... A	resist
2	entreat	.... B	compromise
3	acquiesce	 C	grave
4	disregard	.... D	coarse
5	peevish	.... E	wander
6	vulgar	.... F	enlarge
7	roam	.... G	petulant
8	oppose	.... H	implore
9	amplify	 I	ignore
10	solemn	.... J	comply

Matching pairs 2

1	egotism	.... A	covert
2	grateful	.... B	rugged
3	approach	 C	fixed
4	rough	.... D	overstate
5	immobile	.... E	assiduous
6	imitate	.... F	self-conceit
7	secret	.... G	vanquished
8	exaggerate	.... H	advance
9	persistent	 I	mirror
10	conquered	.... J	appreciative

Answers on page 132

In 2006, a 60 year-old Japanese man set a new world record by reciting pi, that never-ending mathematical number (taught in school as 3.14159), to 100,000 decimal places – from memory in 16 hours. So why do many of us have so much trouble remembering a simple phone number?

Improve your
NUMBER SKILLS

Recalling random sequences of numbers was first devised by a school teacher called Joseph Jacobs in 1887 to measure the mental ability of children in his class, and was used in a similar way by French psychologist Alfred Binet in the early 1900s.

We know that most people can hold between five and nine digits in their working, or short-term, memory. That's why landline phone numbers have seven digits (although there is often an area code to remember as well). People used to commit frequently used phone numbers to long-term memory simply by dialing them over and over again but today automatic and speed-dialling has made many of us more mentally lazy. And few bother to remember

11-digit mobile phone numbers other than their own. So, making the effort to recall other numbers from one day to the next requires strategies.

'Chunking', for instance, breaks down the numbers into groups that are easier to recall. Other techniques involve finding a way to relate to the numbers and link them to other pieces of information so they become meaningful (and therefore memorable), instead of random.

Research shows that using number strategies can improve memory skills tremendously, and scientists have worked hard to find the best technique.

However, research from the Karolinska Institute in Stockholm, Sweden, suggests that there is no single best memory strategy. So experiment and find out what works for you. Once you've done that your memory for numbers will improve significantly.

Smart EVERYDAY STRATEGIES

There are several classic ways to remember numbers beyond the two listed here, but some are very complicated. One involves substituting words for numbers, which takes a great deal of practice. The two below are simple and can be used straight away.

✳ 'Chunk' them

Chunking larger numbers into small groups makes them easier to remember. Try this yourself – look at the following series of numbers for about 5 seconds, then look away and try to write them down in the correct order.

3-7-2-6-9-5-1-8

Now try this again with a different set of numbers. You might find it helpful to say the numbers out loud then say them over to yourself until you can write them down. Look at the numbers for 5 seconds, then look away and try to write them down from memory.

4-6-2　5-3-7　9-8-1

This second time should have been easier, even although there were more numbers (9 instead of 8). Grouping or 'chunking' numbers can help to increase your digit span, and you will probably find that rehearsing or repeating numbers aloud or in your head also helps. This is the reason that telephone numbers are often written out in groups of threes or fours, rather than as a single long string.

✳ Give them meaning

Many mathematicians are particularly good at remembering numbers because they manage to find meaning in them. For instance, show a maths wizard the number 4824 and he might immediately think, four-digit number with the first two digits doubling the second two. If you don't happen to be gifted in this manner, find a different way to relate to the number. For example, a history buff might relate all numbers to significant dates, a librarian may place numbers in the context of the Dewey Decimal System, and a football fan may associate them with a favourite player's numbers or game scores. You can also relate them to the ages and birthdates of family members, or any other numbers you know that come quickly to mind.

If you don't work with numbers in your job, then you probably don't get enough of a chance to become comfortable with them. This is a relatively easy memory category, one that it is perfectly possible to improve. But it is also the one area that can evoke strong responses in some people. If you had bad experiences with maths when you were in school, you may still be suffering from number phobia. Don't worry, you're not going to be tested – these exercises will simply help you to manage the numbers in your life.

HAVE A GO

PIN codes ...

These days, most of us have far too many PINs (personal identification numbers) to remember. Take a look at each of the four PINs below, and try to make an association with the number to help you remember it. To increase the difficulty level, move on to the puzzle, 'Words & numbers' on page 117, before you go to page 116 to see if you can write in the PIN numbers you memorised.

For example: 7613

A person familiar with the song 'Seventy-six trombones' from *The Music Man* might think of that song for the first two digits. Someone with a 13-year-old child might use the child's age to remember the second two.

● PIN code 1
Richard's ATM PIN: 4923

● PIN code 2
Edward's email PIN: 403214

● PIN code 3
Michelle's online banking PIN: 120489

● PIN code 4
Eric's online travel site PIN: 52547

Caller ID ...

Who's calling? Look at the names and phone numbers below. Try to remember which phone numbers are whose. Then turn to page 116 and see how well you do.

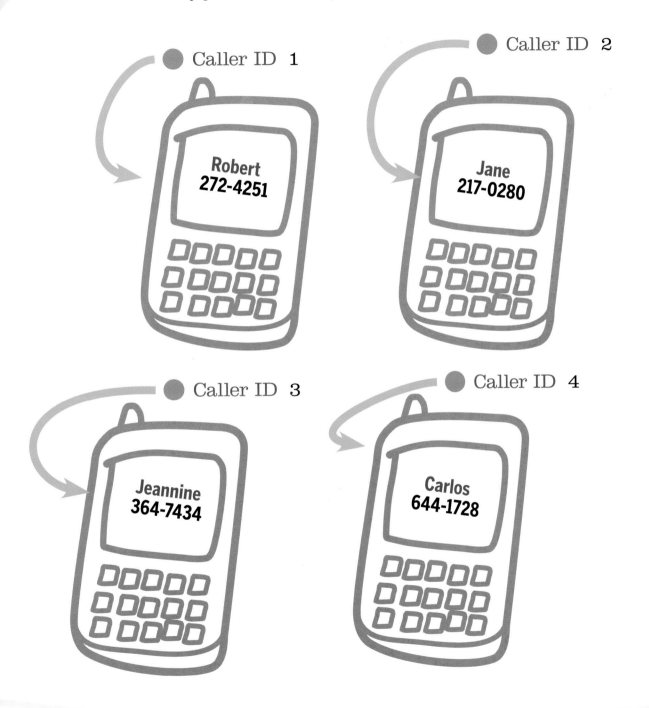

Caller ID 1

Robert
272-4251

Caller ID 2

Jane
217-0280

Caller ID 3

Jeannine
364-7434

Caller ID 4

Carlos
644-1728

PIN codes ...

Write down the numbers you remember, then turn back to page 114 to see how you did.

● PIN code 1
Richard's ATM PIN: ....

● PIN code 2
Edward's email PIN: ....

● PIN code 3
Michelle's online banking PIN: ....

● PIN code 4
Eric's online travel site PIN: ....

Write down the numbers you remember, then turn back to page 115 to see how you did.

● Caller ID 1
272-4251
A Jane
B Carlos
C Robert
D Jeannine

● Caller ID 2
217-0280
A Jane
B Carlos
C Robert
D Jeannine

● Caller ID 3
364-7434
A Jane
B Carlos
C Robert
D Jeannine

● Caller ID 4
644-1728
A Jane
B Carlos
C Robert
D Jeannine

Words & numbers ...

These exercises will help you to
solve everyday problems involving numbers.

● Words & numbers 1

Dan is a full-time university student who has a part-time job. His
girlfriend lives hundreds of miles away. On a particular day, his
classes end at 4pm, after which he immediately drives to his job,
arrives at 4. 15pm, and works for 3 ½ hours, plus a 45 minute
break for dinner. After work, he drives straight home, immediately
starts studying and continues studying for 2 hours and 10 minutes,
and then telephones his girlfriend at 11pm. How long did it take
Dan to drive home from work?

● Words & numbers 2

Dorothy loves entering contests by post. A few years
ago, she bought five books of twelve 39p stamps and
used 15 of them before the first-class rate went up to
41p per letter. If she already has seven 1p stamps and
eight 2p stamps, how much does she have to spend on
additional postage so she can use her remaining 39p
stamps to post her contest entries?

Answers on page 132

Words & numbers ...

● Words & numbers 3

Jacqueline has 15 coins in her purse, all pennies, 20p and 5p pieces. If the total value of her coins is £1.03, how many each of 20p, 5p pieces and pennies does she have?

● Words & numbers 4

A certain airline has a weight limit of 12kg for a piece of carry-on baggage. Marc's empty suitcase weighs 1kg, and he has these items that he'd like to put in it for his flight:

Jar of snacks: 0.5kg
Travel iron: 1.5kg
Crossword dictionary: 1kg
Gift for his mother: 4kg
Laptop computer: 5kg

Which of these items should he take, if he'd like to take as much (by weight) as possible?

Answers on page 132

Sums without symbols …

Place arithmetic symbols **+, -, ÷, ×, =**
(plus, minus, multiplication or division) between the
numbers in each group below to get the result asked for.

For example:

2, 3, 4, 5 to get **19**

Answer:

2 x 3 x 4 – 5 = 19

● Sum 1

8, 6, 4, 11 to get **4**

● Sum 4

15, 5, 11, 6, 5 to get **100**

● Sum 2

10, 3, 8, 2 to get **30**

● Sum 5

5, 4, 2, 4, 6 to get **6**

● Sum 3

9, 2, 8, 4, 10 to get **50**

● Sum 6

12, 2, 8, 4, 3, 4 to get **0**

Answers on page 132

Improve your
REASONING SKILLS

Whether we realise it or not, we use reasoning skills every day. Reasoning actually involves various sets of skills, such as categorising information (that animal looks feline, so it must be a cat), evaluating logic (if that man has only one arm, he wasn't the one who carried the heavy timber into the garage), extrapolation (estimating an outcome from the available evidence) and good old problem solving.

From the time we are old enough to think, our brains start looking for patterns in the seemingly random events of life. We also amass information we can draw on later. Every fact we learn and every problem we solve improves our ability to reason. In that way – experience by experience, decision by decision – we make sense of the world.

The evidence isn't clear about whether we lose the power to think logically and solve difficult problems as we get older, but research shows that everyone – young and old alike – can benefit from training and practice.

If you are not accustomed to doing brain gymnastics, then you may find this section particularly difficult. But remember that challenging your brain is the way to make it more capable. Think of these exercises as interesting puzzles to be solved. If you get tired or frustrated, stop and come back to them another day.

HAVE A GO

Logical or not?

This exercise requires you to pay attention to the story and follow the logic from sentence to sentence. First, read the paragraph and decide if all sentences are logical given the rest of the text. If not, underline the sentence or sentences that don't make sense.

● Puzzle 1

Betty and Bill were having Diane and Dave over that Wednesday evening to hear about their recent holidays, so Bill put a £20 note in his pocket and strolled over to Bestco's, the local grocery store, to pick up a few things that they needed. But Bestco's was closed when he got there – Bill had forgotten that Bestco's closes early on weekends. So Bill had to walk right across town, to the Mammoth Market, to get what he needed. He bought three varieties of cheese, crisps and a bottle of wine. He paid the total cost of £19.75 with his credit card, put everything in the boot of his car and went straight home. As soon as he got home, Diane called to postpone dinner until the following week.

Answers on page 132

Logical or not?

● Puzzle 2

The semi-annual St. Patrick's Day celebration in Ballyhoo is eagerly awaited by one and all. It doesn't matter if you're from Iceland or not, everyone joins in the festivities. The fun starts early in the morning, with the traditional green-egg breakfast (thanks to some food colouring) served in the town square. The parade starts at 10am and lasts for about 2 hours. There is the marching band, of course, with all the flutes, tubas, cellos and trumpets, and elaborately constructed floats on which men in kilts play accordions. The non-musical marchers include representatives from the local schools, civic associations, and the police and fire departments, with the mayor in his green limousine at the very end. Then, everyone rushes to McSweeney's restaurant for the traditional corned beef and cabbage lunch.

● Puzzle 3

Since I've retired, I've become a pretty active user of the internet and get a lot of my news online, but I still like getting the newspaper every weekday morning (I'm much too busy on weekends to sit down with the paper). So my 'newspaper week' starts every Monday morning. The paper arrives like clockwork at 6am, which suits me fine since I'm an early riser. So, with my Monday morning cup of coffee in hand, I read the newspaper from page 1 to the back cover, including the sports news, local and international news, stock-market listings, comic strips and, of course, the daily crossword. After a quick breakfast, I kiss my wife good-bye and take the bus to the office.

Answers on page 132

Puzzle 4

You know what a big tennis fan I am. So it was a happy coincidence that my husband and I arrived in Auckland on July 10th, the day before the Australian Open tennis tournament. As soon as we checked in at our hotel, I took a cab to the stadium, bought tickets for me and my wife, and hurried back to the hotel for dinner.

The tournament is held on two main courts. It's a good thing that they both have retractable roofs, so they can close them if there's rain or it gets too hot. It can be swelteringly hot during the tournament. That night, despite our long tiring journey, I was so excited about the tournament that I couldn't sleep.

Puzzle 5

They call it the waiting room for a reason, you know. Waiting an hour or more to be seen by your doctor is most people's idea of fun. That's why I always bring lots of things to do. Usually, I fill a bag with stuff like knitting, magazines, candles and stationery to catch up on my letter writing. Sometimes, thankfully not too often, there are actually more people waiting than there are seats in the waiting room. When that happens, I walk to the library just a block away and browse the fiction section for the newest books from my favourite authors. The last time I was there, I took out two whodunits, the latest John Grisham legal thriller and a dieting book.

Puzzle 6

Our neighbours recommended Mario's Italian restaurant, which has just opened on the other side of the town. They raved about it: 'Great food, great service, great prices – what more can you ask?' So we had to check it out for ourselves. It really was everything they said it was. We were greeted warmly by Mario himself the moment we walked in the door: 'Welcome back, Mr and Mrs Williams'. The menu was enormous, with five pages of main courses alone. We finally decided what to order. Michele had the veal Marsala, and I decided on the moussaka. The food was great, the portions were huge, and the bill was really reasonable. So we've added Luigi's to our own list of dining favourites.

Answers on page 133

If ...then ...

Clear, careful thinking will help you to solve the logic problems here.

● If ... then 1

Bill's sock drawer has eight pairs of socks in it, each pair has a different pattern, and they're scattered about individually in the drawer. There's a power failure in his home one night, just as he opens the drawer to take out a pair of socks. He takes nine socks out of the drawer, but he can't see them, since the room is dark. Does he have at least one matching pair of socks among the nine?

Answer..............................

● If ... then 2

If in a yearly calendar of events National Egg Month comes before National Peanut Butter Month, National Strawberry Month comes after National Potato Month, and National Potato Month comes after National Egg Month, is National Egg Month before or after National Strawberry Month, or do we not have enough information to tell?

Answer..............................

● If ... then 3

If we know that Brazil has more people than Russia, Russia has more people than Mexico, and Mexico has fewer people than Pakistan, does Brazil or Pakistan have more people, or do we not have enough information to tell?

Answer..............................

● If ... then 4

If Amber's birthday is February 20, and her classmate Amanda was born 10 days later in the same year, do we know what Amanda's birthday is?

Answer..............................

Answers on page 133

If ... then 5

If City B is due east of City A, City C is due north of city B, city D is due south of city B, and City E is due south of City A, what is the direction from City C to City D, or do we not have enough information to tell?

Answer...............................

If ... then 6

A certain restaurant's lunch menu has three choices for sandwiches: tuna fish for £3, chicken salad for £4, and ham for £4.50. Three friends come into the restaurant for lunch, and each one orders a sandwich. If the total cost of the three sandwiches ordered is £10, do we know how many of each sandwich was ordered?

Answer...............................

If ... then 7

If we know that a bushel of wheat weighs more than a bushel of oats, a bushel of barley weighs less than a bushel of sweetcorn, and a bushel of oats weighs more than a bushel of sweetcorn, what weighs more, a bushel of wheat or a bushel of sweetcorn, or do we not have enough information to tell?

Answer...............................

If ... then 8

The fuel tank in Marie's car holds 90 litres (20 gallons). Her car gets 15 miles per gallon in city driving and 25 miles per gallon in motorway driving. If she drives 250 miles on a half-tank of fuel, do we know how many motorway miles and city miles she drove?

Answer...............................

Answers on page 133

Seating plan ...

Kate and Larry are getting married. It's your job to help them design a seating plan for the table at which their relatives will sit – but there are a few restrictions. See if you can figure out who should sit where.

PEOPLE TO SEAT

Kate's Aunt Alice and Uncle Bob (married couple)

Larry's Cousin Carl

Kate's Cousin Dave

Larry's Aunt Ella and Uncle Frank (married couple)

Kate's Uncle George

Larry's Aunt Harriet

Kate's Cousin Ida

Larry's Uncle Jack

SEATING RESTRICTIONS
(in order of importance)

1 All of Kate's relatives sit together, and all of Larry's relatives sit together

2 Married couples must sit together

3 Cousin Dave plays in a rock band and wants to sit as close to the band as possible

4 You're trying to get Cousin Carl to date Cousin Ida, so seat them together

5 Uncle Frank isn't talking to Uncle Jack, so they can't sit next to each other

6 Uncle George owes money to Cousin Dave, so he wants to sit as far from Dave as possible

7 Uncle Bob hasn't seen Uncle George for 20 years, and they have a lot to catch up on

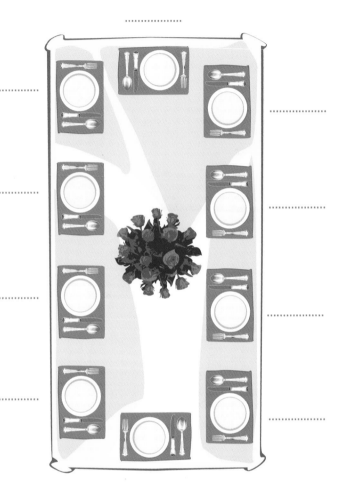

ROCK BAND

Answers on page 133

Next in line ...

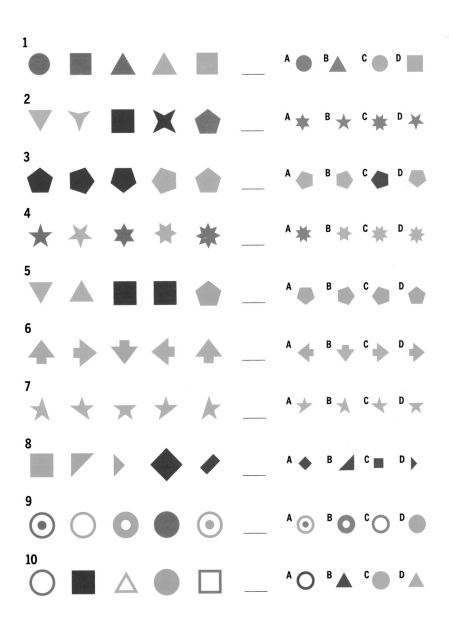

Answers on page 133

ANSWERS

Name that shape 1

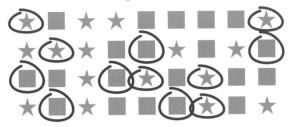

Name that shape 2

Name that shape 3

Name that shape 4

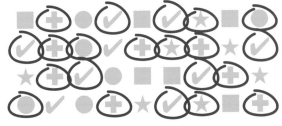

Name that shape 5

Odd one out 1
second row, third item:

Odd one out 2
second row, fourth item:

Odd one out 3
first row, third item:

Odd one out 4
first row, second item:

Odd one out 5
second row, second item:

Odd one out 6
first row, third item:

Spot the difference 1

Spot the difference 2

Spot the difference 3

Spot the difference 4

Picture recall 1

Picture recall 2

Picture recall 3

Letter search 1
43 capitals, 33 lowercase, 6 red

Letter search 2
28 capitals, 30 lowercase, 6 blue

Letter search 3
10 capitals, 32 lowercase, 7 green

Irregular words
1 carrots (not green)
2 brick (not spherical)
3 ostrich (can't fly)
4 rugby (oval ball, no net)
5 inspire (not negative)
6 zebras (don't have dots)
7 camel (can't be a verb)
8 watch (not four letters)
9 money (the only word without the vowel 'a')
10 radio (not something you watch)

Link-up
1 snow **2** year **3** atlas **4** racket **5** ruby **6** buzz
7 colt **8** pothole **9** slither **10** rubber

Circle-grams
1 quality **2** realise **3** deserve **4** pianist **5** cheeses
6 theatre **7** hopeful **8** ominous **9** abdomen

Opposites attract 1
1 e **2** j **3** f **4** i **5** a **6** c **7** b **8** d **9** h **10** g

Opposites attract 2
1 g **2** e **3** h **4** d **5** a **6** j **7** f **8** i **9** c **10** b

Matching pairs 1
1 b **2** h **3** j **4** i **5** g **6** d **7** e **8** a **9** f **10** c

Matching pairs 2
1 f **2** j **3** h **4** b **5** c **6** i **7** a **8** d **9** e **10** g

Words & numbers 1
20 minutes

Words & numbers 2
67p

Words & numbers 3
Eight pennies, four 20p pieces, three 5p pieces

Words & numbers 4
Jar of snacks, travel iron, gift for mother and laptop computer. Total weight: 11kg.

Sums without symbols
1 $8 \times 6 - 4 \div 11 = 4$
2 $10 - 3 + 8 \times 2 = 30$
3 $9 - 2 \times 8 + 4 - 10 = 50$
4 $15 \div 5 + 11 + 6 \times 5 = 100$
5 $5 \times 4 \times 2 - 4 \div 6 = 6$
6 $12 \times 2 \div 8 \times 4 \div 3 - 4 = 0$

Logical or not 1
The store closes early on weekends, but the dinner is on a Wednesday; Bill puts cash in his pocket but pays with a credit card; he walks to the store but puts the items in the car boot.

Logical or not 2
St. Patrick's Day is annual, not semi-annual; it originated in Ireland, not Iceland; cellos are not marching band instruments; men in kilts would play bagpipes, not accordions.

Logical or not 3
There are no stock-market listings on Mondays; the speaker is retired, so he would not go to the office.

Logical or not 4

Auckland is in New Zealand, not Australia; the wife is speaking, yet she buys tickets for her and her wife; July is winter in Australia.

Logical or not 5

'Is' should be 'isn't' most people's idea of fun; one can't use candles in a doctor's surgery; the diet book would not be found in the library's fiction section.

Logical or not 6

The restaurant owner said 'welcome back' but the couple had never eaten there before; moussaka is a Greek, not Italian, dish; the restaurant name is Mario's, not Luigi's.

....

If ... then 1

Yes

If ... then 2

National Egg Month is before National Strawberry Month

If ... then 3

Not enough information to tell

If ... then 4

No.
It could be March 1 (if a leap year) or March 2 (if not)

If ... then 5

City D is due south of City C

If ... then 6

Yes.
Two tuna fish and one chicken salad.

If ... then 7

A bushel of wheat

If ... then 8

Yes.
250 motorway miles.

Seating plan

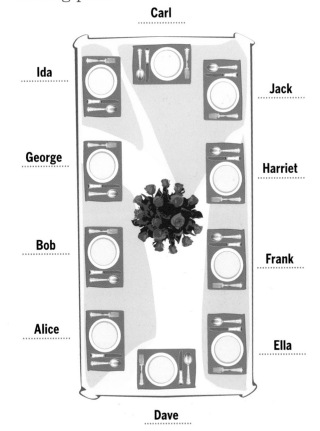

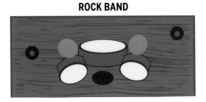

Next in line

1 c **2** b **3** d **4** c **5** a **6** d **7** b **8** a **9** c **10** b

The ten day
JUMP-START PLAN

By now, your brain may be whirling with all the new Sharp Brain ideas and tips you've picked up throughout this book. Perhaps you've already tried a few of the brain-saving tactics. Every minute of every day presents a new opportunity to nourish, nurture and grow your grey matter. But what's the best way to ensure you use those opportunities, now and in the future? Here's a suggestion: start with *The ten-day jump-start plan*.

In the next few pages you'll find a calendar of possibilities to explore. You can do as many or as few as you like but they're all worth trying as each one will benefit your brain in some way. They're not onerous tasks. Scatter blueberries on your breakfast cereal. Make time for a phone call to a friend. Go ten-pin bowling on Saturday instead of watching TV. Guarding your brain against the forces that drain your memory and slow your thinking skills is that simple. The key? Stepping outside your comfort zone just a little bit today … then choosing to do so over and over again in new and different ways. Protecting what goes on in your head also involves tasty brain-healthy foods, good-quality sleep – and plenty of it – fun with friends and family, and time in the great outdoors.

It's all well worth a try to help you get started on the path to an active, challenged brain.

Add zing to your cereal

Sprinkle a handful of blueberries and a tablespoon of chopped nuts onto your breakfast cereal. Voilà! You've just added a helping of brain-protecting antioxidants and good fats to your diet, in less than a minute. That's how easy it is to keep your brain sharp.

Invest in some houseplants

Filling your home – and your outside space if you have one – with flowers and greenery helps to correct 'nature deficit disorder' and gives your brain the contact with nature it craves. It immediately puts you in touch with nature, which some studies suggest can foster sharper recall, quicker reactions and greater creativity.

Prepare to walk

Find your walking shoes or trainers and put them where you'll see them first thing in the morning. You're going for a walk tomorrow.

Get out and about

Lace up your walking shoes and head out the door. A 10 to 15-minute walk is all it takes to boost the flow of oxygen-rich blood to brain cells. And morning sun exposure will help you to sleep better at night so that new memories can be locked into place.

Plan a picnic

If it's summer, start arranging a healthy weekend picnic or barbecue. Plan to include dishes with as many different-coloured fruits and vegetables as you can for an added brain boost. If winter, meet friends for a weekend stroll and then a healthy lunch at a favourite pub.

Get on the phone

Call up an old friend you haven't seen for a while. Have a chat – and before you hang up, make a date for lunch or coffee some time this month. Friendship is one of life's greatest joys … social contact makes your heart sing and your brain thrive.

❋ Sweet fruit, crunchy nuts, healthy oils and satisfying whole grains are part of the Mediterranean diet, which is known to help protect the brain.

Choose brain-friendly oil

Drizzle olive oil on your salad at lunch. Not only does it taste delicious – it offers an important brain benefit. The healthy fats in olive oil can help to reduce inflammation. For an added boost make spinach one of your vegetables today.

Swap tasks

Do a household chore that you always leave to your partner or which rarely gets done. Mow the lawn if you normally scrub the pots; weed the garden if you normally do the dusting. Cross-training your brain in this way builds new connections between brain cells – and your home's ripe with opportunities.

And so to bed …

Put on fresh, clean sheets and get your head down 15 minutes earlier than usual, then stick with your new bedtime all week. A good night's sleep is like a session at a spa for the mind, regenerating brain tissue, preserving memories and even boosting your IQ.

Start with a cuddle

Release the 'cuddle hormone' oxytocin by hugging someone you love (or stroking a beloved pet). As well as giving you a brain boost, it will strengthen your relationships, which helps to lower stress.

Make space for fruit

Take your most attractive fruit bowl or plate and place it prominently on the kitchen table or counter. Fill it with all types of fruit, such as bananas, oranges and rinsed apples and pears. The more colour variety the better. This pretty-as-a-picture centrepiece will have you reaching for antioxidant-packed, brain-nourishing snacks.

Me me me!

Indulge yourself. Soak in a bubble bath, ask your partner for a foot massage, have sex or savour a square or two of delicious dark chocolate (packed with antioxidants). Pleasure raises levels of dopamine, an attention-focusing brain chemical.

❋ **Does walking benefit your brain? Yes! Exercise is like fertiliser for your mind – just a few minutes a day helps brain cell growth.**

Pack the good fats

Put a handful of walnuts into a resealable bag and slip it into your handbag or briefcase to have as your mid-morning snack. Walnuts are full of good fats that improve cell-to-cell communication in the brain.

Say 'hello'

Make time to talk today: have a chat with colleagues, neighbours and friends in person instead of by email or phone. Smile and engage in conversation with shopkeepers. Even brief conversations boost brainpower.

Major on the omega-3s

Serve fish, the ultimate brain food, for dinner. Go for salmon, trout, mackerel or even sardines. All are rich in omega-3 oils, critical for clear thinking, organisation, alertness, learning and reasoning.

Salute the day

Let the sun shine in. Throw open the curtains and pull up the blinds first thing this morning. A dose of early-morning sunlight resets your body clock, boosting mental alertness – which will improve your sleep tonight.

Eat fresh

Shop at a farmers' market or at a nearby supermarket with the biggest fresh produce department. Stock up on a rainbow of brain-friendly and mouth-watering veggies and fruit – then reward yourself with a gourmet salad for lunch or dinner.

Play some nutty games

Gather your family or close friends around the dining-room table for a games night. Brain-teasers such as Scrabble build extra neural connections that protect you from brain decline. Serve a fruity dessert or a platter of sliced fruit and nuts for even more brain benefits.

❋ Your brain loves company. Fun with friends feels great – and people with active social lives tend to suffer less cognitive decline later in life.

Mix it up

Today is 'opposite' day, so step outside your usual routine. Brush your teeth with your non-dominant hand, take a different route to work, or stand when you normally sit. Shaking things up keeps your brain active – and takes it off autopilot.

Soak up the details

Go to a park and pay close attention to everything you see (the shape and texture of the leaves), smell (freshly cut grass), feel (the wind on your face) and hear (birds chirping, children laughing). Flooding your brain with sensory data keeps your grey matter on its toes.

Laugh or learn – or both

See a comedy or foreign film, or, even better, a foreign comedy. A funny film induces brain-healthy laughter, while watching it in a foreign language challenges your brain to keep track of the action and read the subtitles at the same time.

Coffee time

Savour a hot cup of freshly brewed coffee. Studies show that coffee sharpens alertness and boosts processing speed. Not a coffee-drinker? Don't worry; tea also confers brain benefits.

Go vegetarian

Make today a non-meat day. Choose porridge or cereal with dried fruits for breakfast, opt for veggie soup for lunch, then round off the day with some healthy grains such as bulghur wheat or quinoa, topped with beans, lentils or chickpeas in a spicy tomato sauce.

Don't lose touch

Write out a 'call list' of friends, old and new. Starting tonight, catch up with one every day by phone or email. Widening your social circle significantly lowers your risk of cognitive impairment.

❋ Challenging your brain with new experiences keeps it young – the pleasure and surprise puts a sparkle in your eye and a spring in your step.

Walk this way

Add 5 more minutes to your daily walk. From now on, plan to increase your walking time by an additional 5 minutes each week until you're on the go for 30 minutes. Vary your route and explore new places to increase the interest.

Engage yourself

Turn off the TV and lose yourself instead in an absorbing new hobby or project (do a puzzle, read a new book or get out your knitting needles – anything that's different from the norm and gets you in a state of 'flow').

Be thankful

Write down all the good things that happened today. Spending more of your mental energy on gratitude than on worry will help you reduce brain-sapping tension.

Be breath aware

Sit in a comfortable chair in a quiet room for 10 minutes. Close your eyes, pay attention to your breath as it flows in and out, and let your muscles relax. You'll feel refreshed and reduce levels of stress hormones that are toxic to your brain.

Have a massage

Arrange to have a massage – and book yourself in for one next week, and the week after that. If you can't afford it, get into the habit of taking turns with a partner or friend. It helps lower stress levels and reduces pain – good news for your brain.

Treat yourself to more sleep

Turn back your bedtime another 15 minutes tonight, and keep it there. Your mind thrives on a good night's sleep

✻ **Gentle stress-busters – hugging, laughter, relaxation – do more than shield your brain from tension's corrosive effects. They boost your happiness, right away.**

INDEX

digital recorders 69
distractions, controlling 69
doctor, visits to the 69
dopamine 24, 33, 136

E

electronic calendars 82
emotional memory 24, 25
   improvement with age 53
emotional resilience 47
empathy 47, 49
episodic memory 30, 55–6
   declines in 52, 55, 56
errors, recognising 49
events *see* episodic memory
exercise 14, 136
   see also walking
experience
   learning from 47
   sensory experiences 27
   value of 7, 15

F

facts, remembering 30
fallible memory 39
fats, healthy 14, 136, 137
fish 137
flashbulb memory 36, 38
fluid intelligence 42
fMRI scans 19
focus 34, 65
   everyday strategies 69
   exercises 66–8, 70–9
   improving 66–9
   losing 53, 56, 65
   see also attention
forgetfulness, excuses for 29
friendship 135, 138
frontal lobe 22, 44, 45
fruit 135, 136

G

games nights 137
gender differences 33
glia 20
glucose (blood sugar) 29
gratitude 139
grey matter *see* cerebral cortex
grocery lists 107, 108
gut instincts 24

H

headphones 69
hearing tests 99
hippocampus 25, 29, 33, 36
hobbies and interests 7, 139
household chores 136
houseplants 135
hypothalamus 25

I

imaginary memory cues 82
immune system functioning 14
inflammation, reducing 136
information processing *see*
  processing speed
instincts 24
intelligence 15, 41–5
   IQ (Intelligence Quotient)
    Test 41
   lifespan stability of 41
   nature vs nurture 41–2
   seven intelligences 42, 44–5
interpersonal intelligence 45
interpretation 39
intrapersonal intelligence 44–5
intuition 22
IQ (Intelligence Quotient) Test
  41

J

'jamais vu' 24

K

keys, lost 37, 82

L

language 20, 23, 44
laughter 138
learning 7, 13, 31, 33, 34, 35, 42
left and right hemispheres 20,
  44, 45
lifestyle 14
   see also diet; exercise
limbic system 24–5, 96
linguistic intelligence 44
logical-mathematical
  intelligence 44
long-term memory 25, 30–2
   improvement with age 53
longevity 6

M

massage 139
medication side effects 29, 35,
  57, 81
memory
   blocked memories 37
   consolidation 30, 35
   creating memories 12, 32–3
   improving 80–97
   interpretations of events 12
   persistence 33–5
   storage 27–32
   subtotal recall 23
   total recall 13, 53
   see also flashbulb memory;
    long-term memory;
    prospective memory;
    scent memory; semantic

memory; sensory memory; short-term memory (working memory); spatial memory; visual memory
memory cues 82
memory decline
  age-associated forgetfulness 56–7
  dementia 14, 15, 56, 57, 63
  mild cognitive impairment (MCI) 56, 57
  normal/serious 58
memory trails 12, 34
menopause 29
mental agility 12
mental laziness 13, 59
mild cognitive impairment (MCI) 56, 57
'mind-reading' ability 22
misplacing objects 28, 37, 81, 82
mistaken identity 30
mnemonic strategies 106, 107
motor cortex 23, 45
motor skills 23, 32, 45
movement 23, 45
multi-tasking 19, 53, 56
muscle memory *see* procedural memory
musical instruments, learning to play 31, 32, 45
musical intelligence 45
myelin 21

N

names, remembering 23, 30, 34, 38, 107
nature deficit disorder 135
navigation 25, 27, 33
nerve cells *see* neurons
nerve-cell pathways 12, 32–3, 34, 35, 62
neurogenesis 7, 12
neurons 7, 13, 20, 21, 32–3, 42, 56

neurotransmitters 21, 24, 33, 56, 99
new skills, learning 7, 13, 31, 32, 42, 45
newspapers, reading 49
noise control 69
notes, taking 69
number skills 28, 30, 55, 112–19
  chunking 113
  everyday strategies 113
  exercises 114–19
  giving numbers meaning 113
  improving 112–19

O

occipital lobe 23
oestrogen 29
olfactory system 25, 96
olive oil 136
omega-3 fatty acids 14, 137
open-mindedness 47, 49
out-of-the-box thinking 51
oxytocin 136

P

parietal lobe 23, 33, 44
perception 34, 39
personal computer and brain, compared 48
phone numbers, remembering 112–13, 115, 116
physical intelligence 45
physical sensations 23, 25
physical skills 30
picnics and barbecues 135
PIN codes 114, 116
Post-it notes 82
'practice and repeat' 34, 35, 36, 99
prefrontal cortex 22
pregnancy 29

primal urges 24, 25
primary motor cortex 23
problem solving 22, 45, 47
procedural memory (muscle memory) 30, 31–2
  encoding new memories 31
processing speed 13, 53, 56, 98–105
  declines in 99
  everyday strategies 99
  exercises 101–5
  improving 98–105
procrastination 82
prospective memory 32, 59, 81
  declines in 52, 56, 81

Q

quizzes
  brain sharpness 8–10
  wisdom 46, 47

R

reaction time 53, 56
reasoning skills 42, 120–7
  exercises 121–7
recall 37, 38–9, 81
  exercises 83–7, 90–1, 94–5
recognition 81
'remembering to remember' 59, 81

S

scent memory 25, 96
  exercises 96–7
Scrabble 137
self-indulgence 136
self-knowledge 47, 49
semantic memory 30, 55
  improvement with age 56, 59
'senior moments' 28, 30, 56

Cover: Illustration by Samuel Chesterman.

Images repeated throughout: iStockphoto.com/©rambo182 (notepad page/brain hiccups); iStockphoto.com/© Dalibor Rajninger (Bus & car illustrations); iStockphoto.com/© Jason Murray (punching hand/brain power); ShutterStock, Inc/©lineartestpilot (thinking bubble/new thinking).

2-3 iStockphoto.com/© Andrew Rich; 11 iStockphoto.com/© Knape; 16-17 iStockphoto.com/© Andrew Rich; 19 SuperStock Ltd./© Image Source, (Inset) iStockphoto.com/© Julie Felton; 21 Mariana Ruiz/Public Domain; 22-25 © Studio Macbeth; 29 iStockphoto.com/©Nicolas Hansen; 31 iStockphoto.com/Rubber Ball; 34 L ShutterStock, Inc/©Arnoud Quanjer, C ShutterStock, Inc/© Villiers Steyn, R ShutterStock, Inc/© Julia Mihatsch; 37 ShutterStock, Inc/© De2Maraco; 43 iStockphoto.com/© Ekaterina Monakhova; 45 iStockphoto.com/© Soren Pilman; 54 iStockphoto.com/© Marcus Clackson; 60-61 iStockphoto.com/© Andrew Rich; 67 iStockphoto.com/© Rebecca Sabot; 76 Getty Images/© Polkadot Images/Jupiter Images; 77 © Royalty Free; 78 Getty Images/© Image Source Black/Jupiter Images; 79-84 © Royalty Free; 85 T Getty Images/© Thinkstock/Jupiter Images , B Getty Images/© Richard Morrell/Jupiter Images; 86 © Royalty Free; 87 T Getty Images/© Thinkstock/Jupiter Images, B Getty Images/© Richard Morrell/Jupiter Images; 88 TL ShutterStock, Inc/© Africa Studio, TC ShutterStock, Inc/© joingate, TR © Royalty Free, CL ShutterStock, Inc/© IRC, C ShutterStock, Inc/© Gor Leonov, CR ShutterStock, Inc/© Alex Staroseltsev, BL ShutterStock, Inc/© Ivan Ponomarev, BC ShutterStock, Inc/© Eric Isselée, BR ShutterStock, Inc/© objectsforall; 89 TL ShutterStock, Inc/© Stacy Barnett, TC ShutterStock, Inc/© aliola, TR ShutterStock, Inc/© xjbxjhxm123, CL ShutterStock, Inc/© UniqueLight, C ShutterStock, Inc/© Maksymilian Skolik, CR ShutterStock, Inc/© jannoon028, BL ShutterStock, Inc/© R-O-M-A, CB ShutterStock, Inc/© Nadezda, BR ShutterStock, Inc/© fivespots; 90 (A)ShutterStock, Inc/© IRC, (B)ShutterStock, Inc/© Gor Leonov, (C)ShutterStock, Inc/© Eric Isselée, (D) ShutterStock, Inc/© Alex Staroseltsev, (E)ShutterStock, Inc/© Ivan Ponomarev, (F)© Royalty Free, (G) ShutterStock, Inc/© objectsforall, (H)ShutterStock, Inc/© joingate, (I)ShutterStock, Inc/© Africa Studio; 91(A) ShutterStock, Inc/© Nadezda, (B)ShutterStock, Inc/© R-O-M-A, (C)ShutterStock, Inc/© aliola, (D)ShutterStock, Inc/© Stacy Barnett, (E)ShutterStock, Inc/© UniqueLight, (F)ShutterStock, Inc/© xjbxjhxm123, (G)ShutterStock, Inc/© fivespots, (H)ShutterStock, Inc/© jannoon028, (I) ShutterStock, Inc/© Maksymilian Skolik; 92-95 © Royalty Free; 96 ShutterStock, Inc/© Paparazzit; 100 iStockphoto.com/© Eric Gerrard; 101-102 © Reader's Digest/© Rich Kershner; 126 © Adam Raiti; 127 © Dave Phillips; 130 T © Royalty Free, L Getty Images/© Polkadot Images/Jupiter Images, CR Getty Images/© Image Source Black/Jupiter Images; B © Royalty Free; 131 T © Royalty Free, C Getty Images/© Thinkstock/Jupiter Images, B Getty Images/© Richard Morrell/Jupiter Images; 133 © Adam Raiti.

Stay Sharp

Published in 2012 in the United Kingdom by Vivat Direct Limited (t/a Reader's Digest), 157 Edgware Road, London W2 2HR

Stay Sharp is owned and under licence from The Reader's Digest Association, Inc. All rights reserved.

Adapted from *A Sharp Brain for Life* published by The Reader's Digest Association, Inc. in 2011.

We are committed both to the quality of our products and the service we provide to our customers. We value your comments, so please do contact us on 0871 351 1000 or visit our website at **www.readersdigest.co.uk**

If you have any comments or suggestions about the content of our books, email us at **gbeditorial@readersdigest.co.uk**

For Vivat Direct
Project editor Rachel Warren Chadd
Art editor Simon Webb
Senior editor Ali Moore
Senior designer Jane McKenna
Proofreader Maureen Kincaid Speller
Indexer Marie Lorimer

Editorial director Julian Browne
Art director Anne-Marie Bulat
Managing editor Nina Hathway
Trade books editor Penny Craig
Picture resource manager Sarah Stewart-Richardson
Pre-press technical manager Dean Russell
Senior production controller Jan Bucil

Colour origination FMG
Printed in China

ISBN: 978-1-78020-064-4
Book code: 400-578 UP0000-1